THE BIRTHDAY BOOK

THE
BIRTH-
DAY
BOOK

✶

CENSORINUS

Translated by HOLT N. PARKER

University of Chicago Press Chicago & London

CENSORINUS, "most learned in the art of grammar," was
a Roman scholar who wrote *The Birthday Book* in AD 238
as a present for his friend, the Roman knight Caerellius.

HOLT PARKER is professor of classics at the University of Cincinnati.
He has been awarded the Rome Prize, the Women's Classical Caucus
Prize for Scholarship, a Loeb Library Foundation Grant, and a
fellowship from the National Endowment for the Humanities. He has
published on Sappho, Sulpicia, sexuality, slavery, sadism, and spectacles.

The University of Chicago Press, Chicago 60637
The University of Chicago Press, Ltd., London
© 2007 by The University of Chicago
All rights reserved. Published 2007
Printed in the United States of America

16 15 14 13 12 11 10 09 08 07   1 2 3 4 5

ISBN-13: 978-0-226-09974-3 (cloth)
ISBN-10: 0-226-09974-1 (cloth)

Library of Congress Cataloging-in-Publication Data

Censorinus.
[De die natali liber. English]
The birthday book / Censorinus ; translated by Holt N. Parker.
   p. cm.
Includes bibliographical references.
ISBN-13: 978-0-226-09974-3 (cloth : alk. paper)
ISBN-13: 978-0-226-09976-7 (pbk. : alk. paper)
ISBN-10: 0-226-09974-1 (cloth : alk. paper)
ISBN-10: 0-226-09976-8 (pbk. : alk. paper)
I. Parker, Holt N. II. Title.
PA277 . C4D413 2007
878′.01—dc22   2006029081

TO BARBARA

for her Birthday

◦ CONTENTS ◦

⟨ PREFACE ⟩

In the year AD 238, in the capital of the Roman Empire, the scholar Censorinus gave a present to his best friend, the noble Quintus Caerellius. The gift was this charming work, which he called *The Birthday Book* (*De die natali liber*). In its few dozen pages, Censorinus sets down everything related to the idea of birthdays. He begins simply, with the right way to sacrifice to one's Birthday Spirit. By the time he finishes, he has sketched a glorious vision of a universe ruled by harmony and order, where the microcosm of the child in the womb corresponds to the macrocosm of the planets. He is alternately serious and playful. He ranges from the poetic to the pedantic. But everywhere shines his love for learning and for his friend.

The table of contents alone shows the cosmic range of this remarkable book. Almost every subject is included here: math, music, history, astronomy, and embryology. Censorinus gives a short and clear introduction to the science of astrology. He touches on every aspect of time, from a poetic view of infinity to the first sundial at Rome, from the Great Years of the cosmic cycles to the origins of the names of the months. Here are the oldest answers to many of the oldest questions: Did humans evolve from lower life-forms? How does the child grow in the womb? What are planetary aspects? Why does the day begin at midnight? Where did leap year come from? When did the Trojan War begin? Which came first, the chicken or the egg? We find mummies, planets, the size of the earth, the origin of mankind, the Music of the Spheres. And long before our pop psychologists, Censorinus had mapped out the critical passages in life.

The Birthday Book is a vital source for the lost teachings of the Pythagoreans and other Pre-Socratic philosophers, for the vanished books of the Etruscans, and the ancient astrology of the Chaldeans. Censorinus gives the exact date for the heliacal rising of Sirius, the astronomical event that governed the Egyptian year (chapter 21). By comparing all the major calendars of the ancient world, his chronology is one of the anchors for all the dates of ancient history.

The Birthday Book has long been the treasured possession of scientists, poets, and scholars. In the fifth century, the poet and scholar Sidonius Apollinaris praised that "famous volume"; in the sixteenth, the Renaissance genius Scaliger called it "the golden little book." Copernicus studied it; Kepler imitated it. This is its first English translation.

There is even a crater on the Moon named for Censorinus, near the Sea of Tranquility, and explored by *Apollo 10*. It has been called "small but brilliant." It is a perfect tribute to this book.

THE AUTHOR AND THE TEXT

We know little about Censorinus, except what we learn from this book. We know when he was alive, since he tells us the exact year in which he is writing (AD 238, in chapter 13), and that it was after 25 June 238 (chapter 20.10). Priscian (fifth through sixth centuries AD) called him "most learned in the art of grammar" (Priscian *Institutiones* 1.16 = 13.9 ed. H. Keil) and quotes from his book *On Accents.* The family name of Censorinus was an ancient and noble one in Roman history and it is likely that the author was related to L. Marcius Censorinus, censor in 149 BC, whom he mentions in 17.11.

We know a little more about his friend Caerellius, since Censorinus gives us a detailed picture in chapter 15. Caerellius was a provincial who came to Rome, made a name for himself as an advocate, and reached the rank of knight (*eques*). He was older than forty-nine but younger than fifty-six when Censorinus gave him his present (chapter 15.1).

SOURCES AND SCHOLARSHIP

Censorinus is a compiler, not an original scholar. He shows, however, the sorts of wide-ranging and curious learning that was expected of the *grammaticus*, the professional teacher of literature to young men before they began the study of rhetoric.

Censorinus's primary source, whom he praises at several points, is Marcus Terentius Varro (116–27 BC), the great scholar and antiquarian. Censorinus shares material found in the other great encyclopediasts, such as Pliny the Elder, Aulus Gellius, Suetonius, and Macrobius.

Censorinus also has before him a summary of the opinions of the ancient Greek philosophers similar to the one that has come down to us under the name of Plutarch, but which is actually the work of Aëtius (probably late first century AD). This is cited in the notes as Pseudo-Plutarch (Aëtius) *Opinions of the Philosophers* (*Placita*); see *Plutarque: Opinions des philosophes*, ed. Guy Lachenaud (Paris: Les Belles Lettres, 1993); also the edition by H. Deils, *Doxographi Graeci* (Berlin, 1879). Aëtius in turn used Theophrastus's lost *Summary of Opinions about Nature (Phusikôn epitomê)*. J. Mansfeld has argued (in "Doxography and Dialectic. The *Sitz in Leben* of the 'Placita'" in *Aufstieg und Niedergang der römischen Welt* II.36.4: 3179–83, and "Chrysippus and the Placita," *Phronesis* 34 [1989]: 311–42), that Varro did not draw directly on Aëtius, but on an older work, known to Chrysippus and with origins in the Skeptical Academy, which Mansfeld labels the *Vestustissima placita*; for his earlier views, see *The Pseudo-Hippocratic Tract [Peri hebdomadon.]: Ch. 1–11 and Greek Philosophy* (Assen, 1971), 159, 190n198.

MANUSCRIPTS, EDITIONS, AND THIS TRANSLATION

The Birthday Book was always prized for its rare learning and has come down to us through a large number of manuscripts from as early as the beginning of the eighth century AD. See L. D. Reynolds, *Texts and Transmission* (Oxford: Oxford University Press, 1983), 48–50, for details. It was among the earliest books printed in Europe, with a first edition in 1497, and new editions in 1498 and 1500, with eight more in the sixteenth century alone (1514, 1519, 1528, 1567, 1579, 1581, 1583, 1593). I have used the Teubner edition by Klaus Sallmann as the basis of the text: *Censorini De die natali liber ad Q. Caerellium* (Leipzig: Teubner, 1983) and his text with German translation: *Betrachtungen zum Tag der Geburt* (Weinheim: VCH, 1988).

In the translation, I have tried to reflect something of Censorinus's range of styles while keeping within idiomatic English. I have incorporated a few explanatory glosses into the text rather than place them in footnotes, and supplied chapter titles as a guide to the contents, and some diagrams.

I include a basic glossary, plus a few brief notes. Further information can most easily be found in the *Oxford Classical Dictionary*. Censorinus is so admirably clear in explaining even the complexities of astrology and mathematics that he needs little in the way of annotation. The notes are mostly indications of primary sources (with a preference for those that have English translations), and select introductory works in English for readers who might be intrigued by a particular topic. Early Greek philosophers are cited according to the standard numbering system of Hermann Diels and Walther Kranz, *Die Fragmente der Vorsokratiker, griechisch und deutsch* (6. verb. Aufl. Berlin: Weidmann, 1951–52), abbreviated DK. I have not, however, provided the Diels-Kranz numbers for testimonia, which consist only of the bits of Censorinus that readers have in front of them. Generally speaking, I have passed over authors later than Censorinus himself, unless they are especially informative or shed unique light on the text.

My purpose has been to make Censorinus available to English readers. Scholars will wish to consult Sallmann, and the detailed commentaries of Carmelo Rapisarda, *Censorini De die natali liber ad Q. Caerellium* (Bologna: Patron, 1991) and Valter Fontanella, *Censorino: Il giorno natalizio* (Bologna: Zanichelli, 1992–93). There is also a French translation by Guillaume Rocca-Serra, *Censorinus: Le jour natal* (Paris: J. Vrin, 1980). See the review of Sallmann by Anthony Grafton in *Classical Quarterly* 35 (1985), 46–48; also Anthony Grafton and Noel M. Swerdlow, "Technical Chronology and Astrological History in Varro, Censorinus and Others," *Classical Quarterly* 35 (1985), 454–65.

BY CENSORINUS

❁

TO QUINTUS CAERELLIUS:

I ⋆ *Happy Birthday*

1. There are gifts of gold or those that gleam with silver, and gifts more valuable for the decoration than the material. Let the man whom the crowd calls "rich" stare open-mouthed at things of that sort and all the rest of Fortune's favors. Such things have no effect on you, Quintus Caerellius, because you are rich in virtue no less than in money—that is, truly rich. 2. Not that you completely reject the possession or use of riches, but since you have been educated in the discipline of the philosophers, you have realized quite clearly that such things, founded as they are on shifting sands, are neither good nor bad in themselves, but are what the Greeks call "the indifferents," that is, to be considered in between the good and the bad. 3. "Therefore," as the comic poet Terence wrote, "these things are like the soul of the one who possesses them; good for the one who knows how to use them; bad for the one who doesn't use them well." 4. So, since a man is richer not by having more but by wanting less, you have the greatest riches in your soul, which not only exceed the so-called "goods" of the

human race, but even proceed right to the eternity of the immortal gods. For that is what Xenophon, the disciple of Socrates, said: To need nothing is a mark of the gods; to need as little as possible is next to godliness.

5. Therefore, since you have no lack of precious gifts because of the virtue of your soul, and I have no excess because of the thinness of my income, I have sent you this book (take it for what it's worth) composed from my riches, and put the title "Birthday Present" on it. 6. In it I have not, as is most people's custom, borrowed precepts for right living from the ethical branch of philosophy to write to you, nor sought out purple passages from the rhetoricians' handbooks to celebrate your praises. For you have already climbed to such a pinnacle of every virtue that you have excelled in all these things, whether wise admonitions or clever proclamations, by your life and morals. Rather I have chosen certain small problems from the works of the natural philosophers, which gathered together might make up a small volume. 7. I swear I did not do it out of a desire to teach, nor out of a longing to show off, lest the old saying be justly applied to me: "A pig tries to teach Minerva." 8. In fact I know I have learned the most from encountering you, and so that I won't seem ungrateful for all your kindness, I have followed the example of our ancestors, the holiest of men. 9. Since they believed that food, fatherland, light, even their very selves were the gift of the gods, they sacrificed a little of everything to the gods, more to show themselves grateful than because they thought the gods needed it. 10. So when they had harvested the crops, before they ate, they established the custom of offering a libation

to the gods; and whenever they took possession of fields and towns by the gift of the gods, they dedicated a part for temples and shrines where they might worship the gods. Some even, in thanks for continued good health, used to let their hair grow as sacred to the god. 11. In the same way I am paying back to you, from whom I have harvested so much in literature, these small offerings.

2 ⋆ How to Honor the Genius of the Birthday

1. And now, since this is inscribed *The Birthday Book,* let us inaugurate it with all good wishes. So, as the poet Persius said, "Mark this day with a lucky white stone," which I hope you will do as often as possible and, as he added, "Pour out an offering of pure wine to your Genius."

2. Now at this point, someone might ask: "Why *did* Persius think it necessary to pour out unmixed wine for the Guardian Spirit, rather than offering the usual animal sacrifice?" Because, of course, as Varro tells us in his book *Atticus* (the one about numbers), our ancestors held it as a custom and institution, when they paid the Genius his yearly offering on their birthdays, to keep their hands free from slaughter and blood, so that on the day on which they themselves first saw the light, they should not take it away from any other living being. 3. Also, on the island of Delos no one (Timaeus is our authority here) sacrifices a victim on the altar of Apollo the Begetter. This is another strictly observed custom on birthdays: that nobody partakes of the food offered to the Genius before the person who has made the offering.

But now it seems we need to answer the question asked by so many people: "What is a Genius? And why do we venerate him especially on our birthdays?"

3 ⋆ What is the Spirit of the Birthday?

1. A Genius is a god under whose protection each person lives from the moment of his birth. Whether it is because he makes sure we get generated, or he is generated with us, or he takes us up and protects us once we are generated, in any case, it is clear he is called our "Gen-ius" from "gen-eration." 2. Many ancient authors have handed down that the Genius and the Lar, the household god, are the same thing—for example, Granius Flaccus in his book *Formulas for Invoking the Gods,* which he wrote for Julius Caesar. It was believed that the Genius has the greatest, or rather absolute, power over us. 3. Many believed that two Geniuses should be worshipped, at least in married households. Euclides of Megara, the follower of Socrates, however, said that a double Genius has been appointed for each of us, which you can read about in Book 16 of Lucilius's *Satires.* And so we offer special sacrifice to our Genius every year throughout our lives.

4. He, however, is only one of many gods who support human life during everyone's allotted span. The books of formulas for invoking the gods will teach anyone sufficiently who is interested in recognizing them. But all these other gods show the effect of their divinities at only certain points for each person, and so are not summoned with annual religious observances during the entire course of one's life. 5. Our Genius,

on the other hand, has been appointed to be so constant a watcher over us that he never goes away from us for even a second, but is our companion from the moment we are taken from our mother's womb to the last day of our life. But while most people celebrate only their own individual birthdays, I am bound to double duty for this holiday each year. 6. Since from you and your friendship I receive honor, dignity, glory, and protection—in short, all the rewards of life—I consider it a sin if I celebrated your birthday, the day that brought you into the light for me, more casually than my own. For the one day created life for me, but the other created enjoyment and honor for my life.

4 ⋆ *Seed and Conception*

1. Your lifetime starts on your birthday, but there are also many things before that day which pertain to the origin of humankind. It seems relevant, therefore, to say something first about the things which are themselves first in the order of nature. So I shall briefly set out some of the opinions which the ancients held about the origins of mankind.

2. The first and general question treated by the men of old who were learned in wisdom was this: Everyone agrees that individual humans are created from the seed of their parents and in succession propagate offspring, generation after generation. But some authors maintained that there have always been human beings, and that they were never born from anything except human beings, and that there never had been any beginning or starting place to the human race. Others

maintained that there was a time when humans did not exist and that they were allocated a particular point of origin and beginning by Nature.

3. The authorities for the first opinion, that humans have always existed, are Pythagoras of Samos, Ocellus of Lucania, and Archytas of Tarentum, all Pythagoreans; but Plato of Athens, Xenocrates, and Dicaearchus of Messenia and other philosophers of the old Academy seem to have held the same opinion. Also Aristotle of Stagira, Theophrastus, and many other important Peripatetic philosophers wrote the same thing. They gave, as illustration of this fact, a puzzle which they said could never be solved: Are birds or eggs created first, since an egg cannot be created without a bird and a bird cannot be created without an egg? 4. And so they say that for all things in this eternal world, things that always were and always will be, there was no beginning. Instead there is a kind of cycle of things creating and being born, in which the beginning and end of each created thing seem to exist simultaneously.

5. However, there have been many men who believed that the first humans were created by divinity or nature, but they have held very different opinions about it. 6. I will skip over what the fabulous stories of the poets tell: that the first humans were formed by Prometheus out of soft mud or were born from the hard rocks tossed by Deucalion and Pyrrha after the flood. However, some of the professors of philosophy themselves have offered theories in their teachings no less, I won't say monstrous, but certainly no less incredible. 7. For example, Anaximander of Miletus supposed that out of water and earth, after they had been heated, there had arisen fish or fish-like animals, inside of which humans coalesced. They

were retained inside as embryos until puberty; then finally they burst open, and men and women, who were already able to feed themselves, came forth. Empedocles, in his wonderful poem, which Lucretius praised as being so good "that it scarcely seems created by the human race," confirms something of the sort. 8. In the beginning individual members were produced everywhere out of the earth, as if it were pregnant, then they came together and produced the material for a complete human being, composed of fire and moisture mixed. But what is the point of continuing with these improbable things? The same opinion is found in Parmenides of Velia, with the exception of a few small details where he differed from Empedocles. 9. According to Democritus of Abdera, humans were first formed from water and mud. Epicurus is not far behind: he believed that at first "wombs" of some kind grew in the heated mud, clinging to the roots of the earth; children were born out of these and the wombs offered them an organically occurring milky fluid, with nature's help. These original children, when grown and adult, propagated the human race. 10. Zeno of Citium, the founder of the Stoic school of philosophy, held that the origin of the human race lay at the beginning of the world. The first humans were created from the earth with the support of divine fire, that is, the providence of god. 11. Finally, it is commonly believed—by nearly all the genealogical authorities, for example—that the ancestors of various peoples who are not descended from foreign stock were born from the earth, and they are called "autochthonous." This is the case in Attica, Arcadia, and Thessaly. The rough and ready credulity of our ancestors easily believed that even in Italy "Nymphs and native-born Satyrs" held certain forests (as Virgil sang). 12. But nowadays the passion of poetic license has reached such a point that they invent things you can barely listen to, claiming that within the memory of man, long after the various nations were created and cites founded, humans were still being born from the earth in various ways. So in Attica they say that King Erichthonius was born from the seed of Vulcan spilled on the ground; in Colchis and Boeotia, the legend goes that the "Sown Men" came forth fully armed from the sowing of the dragon's teeth; after they killed each other in mutual slaughter, only a few remained who helped Cadmus found Thebes. 13. Also in the area of Tarquinia a divine boy named Tages is said to have been plowed up, who sang poems about the science of reading entrails, which the "Lucumones," priests who ruled Etruria back then, wrote down.

5 ⋆ *Pregnancy*

1. But enough about the origin of humans. Now I will talk as briefly as I can about what pertains to our birth in the present time and its beginning.

2. First, the professors of philosophy do not agree where human seed comes from. Parmenides thought it came at different times from the right and left parts of the body. Hippon of Metapontum (or from Samos, according to Aristoxenus) believed that the seed flows from bone marrow, and thought that his theory was proved by the fact that, if one butchers the males after the animals have mated, no marrow is found, because it has been exhausted, as you might expect. 3. However, many refute this opinion, such as Anaxagoras, Democritus, and Alcmaeon of Croton. They responded that after the mat-

ing of the herds, the males had lost not only marrow but also fat and a great deal of flesh. 4. This question also has raised differing opinions among the authors, whether the fetus is engendered by the seed of only the father, as Diogenes, Hippon, and the Stoics wrote, or also from the mother, as Anaxagoras, Alcmaeon, as well as Parmenides, Empedocles, and Epicurus believed.

6 ⋆ *The Fetus*

5.5. Alcmaeon confessed that he knew nothing for certain about the formation of the fetus, and maintained that no one could learn what formed first in the embryo. 6.1. Empedocles, whose opinion Aristotle followed, judged that the heart formed before anything else, since it contains most of all the life of man; Hippon, however, thought it was the head, in which the ruling essence of the soul is found; Democritus, the belly and the head, the two most hollow parts; Anaxagoras, the brain from which all the senses come.

Diogenes of Apollonia thought that flesh was the first to arise from moisture; then the bones, nerves, and other parts were born from flesh. 2. But the Stoics said that the infant was formed as a whole at a single time, just as it is born and bred. Some believed that it is created by nature herself, so Aristotle and Epicurus; while others attributed it to the power of a spirit that accompanies the seed, so nearly all the Stoics. There are those who hold that there is an ethereal heat in the seed and this forms the limbs, so those who follow Anaxagoras.

3. However the fetus is formed, there are two opinions about how it is nourished in the mother's womb. Anaxagoras

and many others believed that food is provided through the umbilical cord, but Diogenes and Hippon thought that there was a projection in the womb, which the fetus fastens onto with its mouth and through which it draws nourishment, just as it does from its mother's breasts once it is born.

4. Next, these philosophers gave different answers to the question of what causes males or females to be born. Alcmaeon, for instance, said that the child's sex reflected whichever parent supplied the greatest amount of seed. Hippon affirmed that females are born from thinner seed, males from thicker. 5. Whichever parent's essence took hold of the place first had its nature reflected in the child: that was the opinion of Democritus. According to Parmenides, the seed of the female and the seed of the male compete, and the child has the nature of whichever gains the victory. 6. Anaxagoras and Empedocles agreed that males are born from seed flowing from the right parts of the body, females from the left.

Their opinions were in agreement on this point, but quite different on the question of the resemblance of children to their parents. On this question, Empedocles debated the matter and offered the following conclusions. 7. If the heat in the seed of the two parents is equal, a male will be born, resembling his father; if both are cold, a female resembling her mother. If the father's seed is hotter (and the mother's colder), then it will be a boy who will have his mother's face; if the mother's seed is hotter (and the father's colder), then it will be a girl who looks like her father. 8. Anaxagoras, however, judged that children had the face of whichever parent had provided the most seed. Finally, it was the opinion of

Parmenides that when the right parts of the body provided the seed, then children resembled their father; when the left parts, then their mother.

9. Next comes the question of twins. That they are occasionally born, Hippon thought, depends on the quantity of seed: when it is more than enough for a single child, it splits into two parts. 10. Empedocles seems to have thought much the same: he gave no reasons for the division, but said only that it split, and if the places it occupied were equally hot, then two males were born; if both were cold, then two females; if one was hotter and the other colder, then there would be offspring of different sexes.

7 ⋆ Growth in the Womb

1. It remains to speak about the amount of time in which embryos usually mature to the point where they can be born. I will deal with this subject with greater attention, because it is necessary to touch on certain aspects of astronomy, music, and mathematics.

2. First, a question frequently debated among the ancients was in which month after conception children are usually born, but no consensus has been reached. Hippon of Metapontus estimated that babies could be born any time from the seventh to the tenth month. The fetus, he said, was already mature in the seventh month, since the number seven has the greatest power over everything. For we are formed in seven months; after another seven months, we begin to stand upright; after the seventh month, our teeth begin to emerge and then

they fall out in the seventh year; and we usually begin adolescence in the fourteenth year. 3. But this maturity which begins in the seventh month is prolonged to the tenth, because the same natural law applies to everything, so that three months or years are added to the original seven months or years to bring things to completion. 4. So the child's teeth are formed in the seventh month but not completed until the tenth; the first teeth fall out in the seventh year, the last in the tenth; most have reached puberty after fourteen years, but everyone has by seventeen. Some disagree with this opinion in one part and agree with it in another. 5. For many held that a woman can give birth in the seventh month, such as the Pythagorean Theano, the Peripatetic Aristotle, also Diocles, Euenor, Strato, Empedocles, Epigenes, and many others besides, whose unanimous agreement did not prevent Euryphon of Cnidus from boldly denying this very point. 6. Against him, nearly everyone, following the opinion of Epicharmus, has said that a child cannot be born in the eighth month; Diocles of Carystus and Aristotle of Stagira felt otherwise. While most Chaldeans and Aristotle himself thought that a fetus could be born in the ninth and tenth months, Epigenes of Byzantium contended that it was impossible in the ninth, and Hippocrates of Cos denied it could happen in the tenth. 7. Finally, Aristotle alone recognized the eleventh month; all the rest rejected it.

8 ⋆ *The Origins of Astrology*

1. And now the system of the Chaldeans needs to be treated briefly, and an explanation given of why they believe that humans can be born only in the seventh, ninth, or tenth month.

2. Before all else, they say, our actions and lives are under the influence of the fixed and the movable stars. The human race is governed by their varying and complex motion, and in turn the stars' and planets' own motions, configurations, and influences are frequently affected by the sun. For the power of the sun causes some to have their risings, others to have their fixed positions, and makes the planets affect each of us with their individual temperaments. 3. And so the sun moves the stars by which we are moved in turn; it gives us the spirit by which we are ruled; it is most powerful over us and controls how long after conception we are born. And it does this by means of three "aspects."

I'll say a few things first about what "aspect" means and how many kinds there are, so you can understand it as clearly as possible. 4. There is a circle that, as they say, "bears the signs." The Greeks call it the *zodiac*. The sun, moon, and the other wandering stars are carried within it. It is divided into twelve equal parts, one for each sign. The sun measures it out in its annual journey, and so spends approximately one month in each sign. Each sign has a mutual "aspect" with each other sign, though not the same with each one: some are considered stronger, others weaker. Now at the time when a child is conceived, the sun is necessarily in a sign and in a precise subdivision of that sign, which they call the "Place of Conception." 5. Each sign has thirty of these "degrees," and so a total of 360 degrees in the entire zodiac. The Greek call these degrees *moirai,* that is, "lots," no doubt because they call the goddesses of Fate "The Moirai." And indeed these degrees are like fates to us, for the one which is rising as we are born has the greatest power over us.

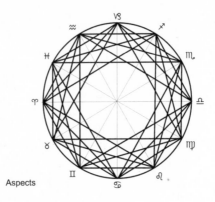

Aspects

6. The sun, therefore, when it passes into the next sign, either "looks" at the Place of Conception with a weak aspect or does not look at it at all. For many have denied that neighboring signs of the zodiac look at each other in any way.

However, when the sun is in the third sign, that is, with one sign in between, then for the first time it is said to "look" at the place it set out from, but only with an oblique or weak light.

This aspect is called the "hexagonal" because it subtends the sixth part of the circle; that is, if lines are extended from the first sign to the third, then to the fifth, seventh, and so on, the form of an even-sided hexagon is inscribed in the circle. 7. However, the Chaldeans did not take this aspect into account in every situation, because it seemed to have little to do with the growth of the fetus.

8. However, when the sun passes into the fourth sign and there are two in between, it looks with the "square" aspect, because the line which stretches between the two signs now

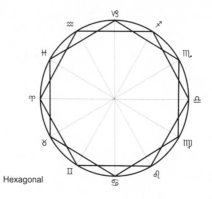

Hexagonal

cuts off the fourth part of the arc. 9. When the sun passes into the fifth sign and there are three signs in between, then the aspect is "triangular," because that sight line measures out a third of the zodiac.

These last two aspects, the square and triangular, are very powerful and minister especially to the growth of the fetus. 10. The next aspect in the sixth place lacks any power, because its line does not form the side of any polygon. However, the aspect from the seventh sign, the one directly opposite, is the fullest and most powerful. It brings forth some children already mature, who are called "seven-month" children because they are born in the seventh month. 11. But if the womb is not able to bring the child to maturity within this period of time, it is not born in the eighth month, for the aspect from the eighth month, like that of the sixth, is unproductive, but rather it is born in the ninth or tenth. 12. For the sun looks back from the ninth month to the Degree of Conception in the triangular aspect and from the tenth in the square aspect, and these two

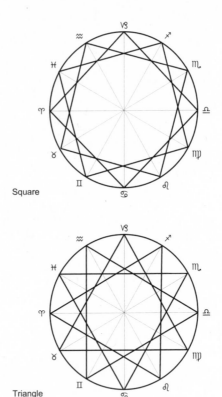

Square

Triangle

aspects, as was said above, are the most productive. 13. Finally, children cannot be born in the eleventh month, because the weak "hexagonal" aspect is formed, with a ray by now powerless; much less in the twelfth, which creates no aspect. And so in this theory, seven-month children are born "on the diameter," nine-month children are born "on the square," and ten-month children are born "on the triangle."

9 ★ The Teachings of the Pythagoreans

1. Now that the beliefs of the Chaldeans have been explained, I pass on to the opinion of the Pythagoreans as set forth by Marcus Terentius Varro in his book *Tubero,* subtitled *On the Origin of the Human Race.* 2. This theory can be accepted as particularly credible, since it comes closest to the truth. Many other philosophers, despite the fact that all children do not come to term after the same amount of time, have nonetheless assigned a single period of time for the formation of them all. So Diogenes of Apollonia, who said that it takes four months for the body of male children to form and five for females; or Hippon, who wrote that a fetus is formed in sixty days, the flesh becomes solid in the fourth month, the nails and hair begin to grow in the fifth, and the human being is already complete in the seventh.

3. Pythagoras, however, said something more believable: that there are two types of pregnancy, one of seven months, the other of ten, and the first corresponds to one set of numbers, the second to a different set. These numbers cause change in each fetus, determining when semen turns into blood, blood into flesh, and flesh into human form, and when they are compared to each other, they have the ratios called "voices," which in music are known as "harmonies."

10 ★ Harmony and Music

1. But in order that these things might be more easily understood by the intellect, certain things must be said first about the rules of music, especially since the things I will say are

unknown even to musicians themselves. 2. For they have learnedly discussed sounds and reduced them to a regular sequence, but the mathematicians have discovered more about the modes and measurement of the motions in sounds themselves than musicians have.

3. Music, then, is the art of regulating sounds well. The starting point is the voice; the voice sometimes comes out low, sometimes high; voices, however produced, that are single sounds are called "notes." The difference between two notes, one higher, one lower, is called the "interval." 4. One can divide the space between a low sound and a high sound into many regular intervals, some larger, some smaller, such as that which they call the "tone," or the smaller "semitone," or else an interval of two, three, or any number of tones. But not every sound joined in a haphazard fashion with any other sound produces concordant effects in song. 5. Just as our letters, if they were joined together randomly and incorrectly, would seldom unite to form words or syllables, so in music there are certain fixed intervals which are able to produce "harmonies." 6. Harmony is the union of two different notes that sound pleasant when played together. There are three simple and primary harmonic intervals from which the others derive: the first, having the interval of two and a half tones, is called the "fourth"; the second, of three and a half tones, is called the "fifth"; the third is the "octave," whose interval contains the first two. 7. The octave is calculated as six tones (as Aristoxenus and the musical theorists maintained) or five full tones plus two semi-tones (so Pythagoras and the mathematicians, who pointed out that two semi-tones do not necessarily add up to a full tone. Plato incorrectly called an interval of this

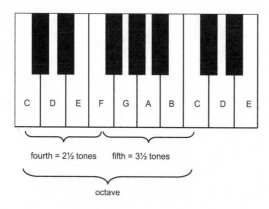

fourth = 2½ tones   fifth = 3½ tones

octave

type a "semi-tone," elsewhere more properly the *dialeimma,* or "leftover").

8. Now in order to show clearly how sounds, which are subject neither to the eyes nor the touch, can have "measurement," I will discuss the wonderful invention of Pythagoras, who discovered the secrets of nature by observing that the musicians' "notes" corresponded to numerical ratios. For he stretched strings of equal thickness and equal length with different weights. He plucked them repeatedly and changed the weights on the ones whose notes did not produce any harmony together.

He did this again and again until he finally discovered that two strings produced an interval of a musical fourth when their weights had the same ratio as three does to four, which the Greek mathematicians call *epitrite,* and the Roman mathematicians call "four-thirds." 9. The harmony called the fifth, he discovered, resulted when the weights were in the proportion which we call "half again as much," that is the ratio of

Pythagoras's experiments from Franchinus Gaffurius,
Theoria Musicae (Milan, 1492)

two to three, which the Greeks call *hemiolon*. Finally, when one string was stretched with twice the weight of the other, the ratio called "double," it sounded the octave.

10. He tried to see if this would work with flutes and found exactly the same thing. He set up four flutes with equal diameter but different lengths. The first was, say, six fingers long; the second was a third longer, i.e., eight fingers; the third was nine fingers, i.e., one and a half times longer that the first;

and the fourth was twelve fingers, doubling the length of the first. 11. When these flutes were blown, and compared two by two, the ears of all the musicians agreed the first and second produced the same interval as the musical fourth, and that the proportion was three-quarters; between the first and the third flutes, where the ratio is one and a half, there sounded a fifth; and the interval of the first and the fourth flute, which had a double ratio, produced the octave. 12. But there is a difference between the nature of the strings and the nature of the flutes, for an increase of length makes the flute lower in sound, but an addition of weight makes the strings higher. Nevertheless, the ratio remains the same.

11 * Harmony in the Womb

1. Now that I have explained these things, somewhat obscurely but as clearly as I could, let me return to my main argument and teach what Pythagoras thought about the number of days involved in childbirth.

2. First, as I mentioned before in general terms, he said that there are only two types of pregnancy, the shorter one called the seven-month, where the child comes forth from the womb on the 210th day after conception; the other is longer, the ten-month, and the child is born on the 270th day. Of these, the first and shorter one is based on the number six.

3. According to Pythagoras, what is conceived from the seed is for the first six days a milky humor, then bloody for the next eight; when these eight days are compared to the first six, they form the first harmony, known as the "fourth," i.e., 3:4. In the third stage, nine days are added, now making flesh; these

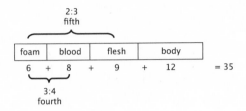

compared to the first six make the ratio 2:3, the second harmony, the "fifth." Then finally, after a subsequent twelve days,
the body becomes fully formed; the comparison of these with
the same six makes the third harmony called the "octave," in
the ratio 1:2. 4. These four numbers—6, 8, 9, 12—when added
produce 35.

And so the number six is the basis of conception, and for
good reason. The Greek call it *teleion* (we say "perfect"), since
it has three parts: a sixth, a third, and a half, that is, one, two,
and three, making the very same thing [i.e., $1/6 + 1/3$ ($2/6$) +
$1/2$ ($3/6$) = 1; and $1 + 2 + 3 = 6$]. 5. At the beginning of the
process, the initial stage of seed (the milky basis of conception), is brought to completion by the number six. Likewise,
the thirty-five days of the next stage, that of the fully-formed
human being (which one might call the second starting point
for growth), when multiplied by the number six, produces the
fully-grown child when it reaches the 210th day.

6. The other pregnancy, the longer, is contained by the
larger number, i.e., seven, by which all of human life is bound,
as Solon wrote. The Jews follow this in numbering all their
days, and the ritual books of the Etruscans seem to indicate
this too. Hippocrates and the other doctors point to the same

thing in the bodies of the sick, for they considered each seventh day to be "critical," that is a "crisis" day.

7. So just as the origin of the first type of pregnancy is in six days, after which the seed turns into blood, so the origin of this second type is based on seven. And as in the first case the infant becomes articulated in thirty-five days, so here following the ratios it becomes articulated in about forty days. (That, by the way, is why in Greece they consider fortieth days special. For example a pregnant woman cannot appear in a sacred area before the fortieth day, and for forty days after birth the majority of mothers are sick and lose blood occasionally, while the children are weak for about the same number of days, sickly, without smiles, and not without danger. For that reason, when this day is past, they celebrate a holiday which is called "Fortieth Day.")

8. So these forty days multiplied by the initial seven give 280 days, that is, forty weeks; but since the child is actually born on the first day of the last week, six days are subtracted and the result is 274 days. This number of days corresponds perfectly with the "square" aspect of the Chaldeans. 9. For the sun travels around the zodiac in 365 days and some odd hours. When a quarter is subtracted, that is, ninety-one days and a few hours, it must run through the other three-quarters in not more than 274 days until it comes to the spot where it looks toward the Place of Conception with the square aspect.

10. No one need wonder how the human intellect has been able to observe these days of change and examine the secrets of nature. The experience of the doctors has frequently observed these things, for they have noticed that many women do not retain the seed which was taken in, and know for a fact

that what is ejected within six or seven days is milky, and they call it "efflux," and what is ejected later is bloody and called "miscarriage."

11. The fact that both types of gestation seem to be contained by even numbers, while Pythagoras approved only odd numbers, does not contradict the doctrines of the sect. He explained that only an odd number of *full* days was completed, 209 and 273 respectively, but a small portion of the following days was added for completion; this portion, however, still does not add up to another full day. 12. We see that nature has followed a similar pattern in the length of the year and month, for it has piled on a small amount to the odd number of days in the year, 365, and added a little something to the twenty-nine days of the lunar month.

12 ⋆ Harmony in the Mind and Body

1. It is perfectly believable that music has a relation to our birthdays. For whether music is only in the voice (as Socrates said), or in the voice and the motions of the body (following Aristoxenus), or in them both as well as the motion of the soul (as Theophrastus thought), in any case it has much of the divine in it, and has the greatest power to move souls. 2. For if music were not pleasing to the immortal gods, who consist essentially of divine spirit, then festivals with plays and music would not have been instituted in order to please the gods; a flute player would not accompany all prayers in sacred temples; the triumph for Mars would not be celebrated with a flute player; the lyre would not be the attribute of Apollo, nor would flutes and other musical instruments be the attributes

of the Muses; flute players, whose purpose is to please the gods, would not be allowed to open the games and to be fed at public expense on the Capitoline Hill, or to wander the city during the Little Festival of Minerva on the Ides of June [13 June], dressed however they like, in masks, and drunk.

3. The human mind, which is itself divine (though Epicurus disagreed), recognizes its divine nature through song. When a ship is underway, the steersman gives his crew harmony to lighten their labors, and when the legions are fighting on the battle lines, the fear of death is driven back by the trumpet. 4. This is why they say Pythagoras always sang with a lyre before he went to sleep and after he got up, so that he could imbue his soul with its own divinity; and Asclepiades, the doctor, restored the insane, deeply disturbed by some illness, to their right minds with harmony. Indeed, Herophilus, the great practitioner of the art of medicine, said the pulses in the blood vessels move to musical rhythms. 5. And so if there is harmony in the very motions of our body and soul, there can be no doubt that music is connected to our birthdays.

13 ⋆ Harmony in the Universe

1. In addition to all these things, Pythagoras asserted that the whole universe is made according to musical ratios; that the seven planets, which control the nativities of mortals, as they wander between earth and heaven, have motions called "harmonic," and the distances between them correspond to musical intervals; and that they give off different sounds in accordance with their altitude, and so sing in chorus the sweetest melody possible, but inaudible to us because of the highness

of the notes, music which the limitations of our ears cannot capture.

2. Just as Eratosthenes figured out by geometrical calculation that the full circumference of the Earth is 252,000 stadia [about 29,060 miles], so too Pythagoras indicated how many stadia there were between the Earth and each planet. (The stadium used in this particular measurement of the Earth, it must be noted, is the one called the Italic, which is 625 Greek feet long [about 610 English feet]. There are others which differ in length, such as the Olympic stadium, which is 600, and the Pythian, which is 1000 feet.) 3. Pythagoras thought that from the Earth to the Moon was about 126,000 stadia [about 14,530 miles], and that this was the interval of a tone; from the Moon to the planet Mercury, which is called Stilbon, was half that, or a semi-tone; from there to Phosphoros, i.e., the planet Venus, about the same, another semi-tone; and from there to the Sun, three times as much, that is, one and a half tones. 4. So the Sun is three and a half tones away from the Earth, that is a musical fifth, and two and half tones away from the Moon, that is a musical fourth. Continuing, from the Sun to the planet Mars, whose name is Pyrois, is the same interval as from the Earth to the Moon, a tone; from there to the planet Jupiter, which is called Phaethon, half the distance, producing a semi-tone; the same from Jupiter to the planet Saturn, whose name is Phaenon, i.e., another semi-tone; and then to the highest heaven, where the constellations are, another semi-tone. 5. And so the interval from highest heaven to the Sun is a fourth, i.e., two and a half tones, and from heaven to the surface of the Earth there are six tones, which make a harmonic octave.

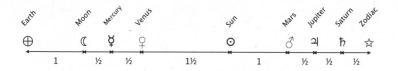

Pythagoras's Cosmos

Pythagoras applied many things that the musical theorists deal with to the other stars, and showed that the entire universe is "harmonic." That is why Dorylaus wrote that the universe is the musical instrument of God. Others have added that it is a seven-stringed lyre, because there are seven wandering stars, which move especially. 6. But this is not the place for all these things, which need precise treatment, and even if I wanted to gather them in a separate volume I still would not have enough room. Rather, since the sweetness of music has led me far away, let me return to my topic.

14 ⋆ Crisis Years and the Length of Life

1. Now that what happens before our birthday has been explained, I want to talk about what we can know about the stages of human life, in order to recognize the "climacteric" years.

2. Varro thinks that our life span is divided into five equal stages, each one fifteen years long, except the last. In his scheme, those in the first stage, up to age fifteen, are called boys (*pueri*) because they are "pure" (*puri*), that is, sexually immature. In the second, up to age thirty, they are "adolescents," so called from "growing up" (*adolesco*). In the third stage, those

who are up to forty-five years old are called "youths" (*iuvenes*), because they are able to help (*iuv-are*) the state in military matters. In the fourth, up to age sixty, they are called "seniors," because then the body first begins to grow old (*senescere*). From that point to the end of each one's life forms the fifth period. Those in it are called "old men" (*senes*) because the body at this age already labors under senility (*senium*).

3. Hippocrates the doctor distributed the ages into seven stages. The end of the first period, he thought, was the seventh year, the second ended at fourteen, the third at twenty-eight, the fourth at thirty-five, the fifth at forty-two, the sixth at fifty-six, and the seventh at the last year of human life. 4. Solon made ten parts, dividing Hippocrates' third, sixth, and seventh stages into two, so that each age had seven years. 5. Staseas the Peripatetic added two more periods of seven years to Solon's ten, and said the length of a full life was eighty-four years; he said that if anyone went beyond this limit, he did the same thing that Olympic runners and charioteers do when they continue running beyond the finish line. 6. Varro writes that in the Etruscan books of fate a person's lifetime is separated into twelve groups of seven. Life [the text is missing a few words—*Trans.*] could be extended to the tenth group of seven years by begging to postpone the fated moment with sacrifices, but from the seventieth year onwards it was neither suitable to beg nor possible to obtain this from the gods. Finally, after eighty-four years people begin to lose their mental faculties, and no more signs of divine favor are given them.

7. Of all these people, those who measure out human life into sevens seem to have gotten closest to Nature, for it is after each interval of approximately seven years that Nature

shows us some turning point, and something new occurs during them. You can learn this also from Solon's famous elegy. He says that in the first seven years a person's baby teeth fall out; in the second, pubic hair appears; in the third, the beard grows; in the fourth, strength; in the fifth, the maturity necessary to leave behind offspring; in the sixth, one becomes more moderate in one's desires; in the seventh, wisdom and tongue reach perfection; in the eighth, they stay strong (others say the eyes begin to go); in the ninth, everything becomes weaker; in the tenth, man becomes ready for death.

[A few sentences are missing . . . Other philosophers add various things about the different stages, especially the first seven years.—*Trans.*] . . . although in the second group of seven years or at the beginning of the third, the voice breaks and becomes deeper, which Aristotle called to "goat-ize" and our ancestors called "to go goaty." They thought that young boys were called "billy goats" because the body begins to smell like a goat. 8. In Greece, they subdivide the third age, that of the adolescents, before the boys come to manhood, into three stages: they call the fourteen-year-old, "child"; the fifteen-year-old, "pre-ephebe"; the sixteen-year-old, "ephebe"; and the seventeen-year-old "post-ephebe."

9. Besides these, there are many facts about the number seven which doctors and philosophers have set down in books, from which one learns that in diseases, for example, every seventh day is dangerous and is called "crisis." In the same way during one's entire lifetime, every seventh year is dangerous and called "critical" and "climacteric." 10. However, the astrologers have said that some of these are even more dangerous than others. Many authorities say that the most

important ones to watch out for are those which end a group of three sevens, i.e., the twenty-first, the forty-second, the sixty-third, and finally the eighty-fourth, which Staseas made the finish line of life. 11. A number of others, however, single out one particular year as the most difficult climacteric of all, namely the forty-ninth, which is the product of seven times seven years. Majority opinion inclines to this theory, because square numbers are said to be the most powerful. 12. Let me call as witness Plato, the most blessed figure in ancient philosophy, who thought that human life reached its final stage in a square number, but it was the square of nine, eighty-one years. There were also some who admitted both numbers, forty-nine and eighty-one, ascribing the smaller number to those born at night, the larger to those born during the day. 13. Many have cleverly divided up these two sets of numbers, saying that the sevens apply to the body, the nines to the spirit; seven is attributed to medicine of the body and to Apollo, but nine to the Muses, because we usually soothe and cure mental disease, which the Greeks call *pathos,* with music. 14. Therefore they have handed down that the first climacteric year is forty-nine, the third and last is eighty-one; the one in between is composed of both, sixty-three, which is nine times seven or seven times nine. 15. Although some say that this is the most dangerous year, because it applies to both the body and the soul, I think it is less powerful than the other two. It is the product of the two aforementioned numbers, seven and nine, but it is the square of neither, and although it is related to both, it has power over neither. Nor do I find that many people who were famous in antiquity have been carried off in their sixty-third year. 16. There is Aristotle of Stagira, but they say he was subject to a natural weakness of the stomach and frequent attacks of pain in his sickly body, which he endured so long only by the power of his soul, so that is it more amazing that he put up with his life for sixty-three years than that he did not put off his death longer.

15 ⋆ *The Praise of Caerellius*

1. Therefore, most blessed Caerellius, since you have passed that forty-ninth year which held the greatest danger for your body without any problem, I am less afraid of the other minor climacteric years for you, especially since I know that in you the natural force of the soul is more the master than the force of the body, and men who were like that of old did not pass from this life until they reached eighty-one, the year which Plato thought was the proper end of life (and held himself to it!). 2. In that year Dionysius of Heraclea abstained from food in order to leave his life, and Diogenes the Cynic, in the opposite way, was undone by a bilious attack brought on by overeating. Eratosthenes, the man who measured the globe, and Xenocrates, the follower of Plato and head of the old Academy, lived to that same year. 3. There are even several who surpassed this limit, as the weakness of their bodies was conquered by the power of their spirit, such as Carneades, head of the Third or New Academy, who lived to be ninety, or Cleanthes, who made it to ninety-nine. Xenophanes of Colophon was more than a hundred years old. Democritus of Abdera and Isocrates the orator, they say, almost reached

the same age as Gorgias of Leontini, who, as is well known, was by far the oldest of the men of antiquity and lived to be one hundred and eight.

4. Therefore, if these lovers of wisdom gained a long life through the virtue of their souls or the law of fate, I have no doubt that you will continue to flourish in both body and soul, and that an even longer old age awaits you. For who among the ancients, whom we hold in memory, can we say was superior to you in wisdom, self-control, justice, or fortitude? Which of them, if he were here, would not confer on you the winner's proclamation in all the virtues? Who would blush to be in second place after your praises? And what is most worthy of proclamation, in my opinion, is the fact that nearly all of these men, although very wise and far removed from public affairs, were unable to live their lives without insult and in many cases deadly hatred, while you, who have enjoyed civic offices, who are distinguished for the honor of the priesthood paid you among the leaders of your city, who have passed beyond provincial status into the dignity of the Roman equestrian order, you have always lived not only without reproach or envy, but also have gained the love of everyone in every way, together with the greatest glory. 5. Which member of the noblest order of the Senate does not strive to be recognized by you? Who of the lower order of the common people does not hope the same? What mortal has seen you or even heard of your name without loving you like a brother and honoring you like a father? Who does not know that the greatest honesty, highest faithfulness, incredible kindness, remarkable modesty and respectfulness, and all other virtues of culture

and kindness become one in you, virtues greater than can be justly praised by anyone? 6. And so I too must now leave untouched things which ought to be commemorated. Even about your eloquence I am silent, since every tribunal of our provinces and every governor knows it, and ultimately the city of Rome and Very Important Audiences have wondered at it. Your eloquence needs no help to ennoble itself to this, as to future ages.

16 ⋆ *Time and Eternity*

1. But now since I'm supposed to be writing about birthdays, I will attempt to complete my gift, and indicate with the clearest possible signs the present time in which you flourish, and thereby make known exactly that first day of your birth.

2. By "time" I don't mean just a day, a month, or the turning year, but also what some call the *lustrum* or "Great Year," and also what they call a *saeculum,* an "age," or "cycle." 3. About the "Eon," the largest single period of time, I am not going to say much at present. It is immeasurable, without origin, without end. It was and always will be the same duration. It does not affect one man more than another. 4. It is divided into three periods: past, present, future. Of these, the past lacks a beginning, the future lacks an end, and the present, in between them, is so thin and ungraspable that it has no length and seems to be nothing other than the meeting point of what has been and what will be. It is so unstable that it is never in the same place, and it takes whatever elapses from the future and adds it to the past. 5. These two "times" (I mean

that which has happened and that which is to come) are not equal, and yet not such that one seems longer or shorter than the other, for that which has no end admits no comparison of measurement. 6. So I will not try to measure the Eon by a number of years or of centuries, nor any unit of finite time. For these, in comparison to infinite time, are not equal to one short hour in winter.

17 ⋆ Ages and Centuries. The Roman Secular Games

16.7. And so that I can run through the ages and mark out this our present age, I will skip the Ages of Gold and Silver and other such poetic stuff, and begin with the founding of Rome, our common Fatherland. 17.1. And since "ages" are either natural or civil, I'll speak first about the natural ones.

2. An "age" (or *saeculum*) is the longest period of human life, delimited by birth and death. So those who think that thirty years is an "age" seem to be way off. Heraclitus is the authority for calling this length of time a "generation" (Greek *genea*), because there is in it a circle of a lifetime. He calls it the "circle of a lifetime" because nature runs from one human "sowing" to the next "sowing." Others define the time period "generation" differently: Herodicus writes that twenty-five years is called a generation; Zenon, thirty. 3. In my opinion, how long an "age" lasts has not yet been closely examined. Poets, of course, have written many unbelievable things, but then so have the Greek historians, who do not have the right to depart so far from the truth; for example, Herodotus, in whose *History* we read that Arganthonion, King of Tartessus, lived to be 150 years old; or Ephorus, who wrote that the Arcadians say that among them

certain kings at certain times lived 300 years. 4. I am skipping these things as fictional.

But even among the astronomers, who search for truth in the order of the planets and constellations, there is no agreement. Epigenes laid down that the longest human life was 112 years; but Berosus, 116. Others believed it could extend to 120, others even further. There were some who thought that a single figure was not to be observed everywhere, but that it varied in different regions according to the inclination of the heavens to the circle of the horizon, which is called "climate."

5. Although the truth lies hidden in darkness, nevertheless the ritual books of the Etruscans seem to teach what the natural ages are in each society, in which they say it is written that the beginning of each Age is determined as follows. Starting from the day on which the particular cities and states were founded, out of those who were born on that day, the day of death of the one who lived the longest marks the end of the First Age. Next, out of those who were alive in the state on *that* day, in turn the day of death of the person who lived the longest is the end of the Second Age, and so the duration of the rest of the Ages is marked off. But due to human ignorance, certain portents are sent by the gods to show when each Age is over. 6. The Etruscans, who have experience in their special science of reading omens, watched for these portents diligently and entered them in books. So the Etruscan Chronicles, which were written in their Eighth Age, as Varro tells us, contain not only how many Ages were given to that people, but also how long each of the past Ages was, and what signs marked their ends. And so it is written that the first four Ages were 105 years long; the Fifth was 123 years; the Sixth

and Seventh were 119 years; the Eighth Age was still going on; the Ninth and Tenth remained; and after these were over would come the end of the Etruscan name.

7. Some think that the Roman "age" or *saeculum* is marked by the Secular Games. If we could believe this, it would mean that the time span of the Roman *saeculum* or "century" is variable, since when it comes to the intervals at which the games ought to be held, we are ignorant not only of how long they were in the past but also how long they ought to be now. 8. We have it on the authority of Antias and other historians that they were originally founded to occur every hundred years. Varro wrote the same thing in Book I of *The Early Theater at Rome:* "Since there were many portents, and both the wall and tower between the Colline and the Esquiline gates were touched by heaven, the Council of Fifteen consulted the Sibylline books and announced that the Tarentine Games should be held in the Field of Mars in honor of Father Jupiter and Persephone for three days, and that black animals should be sacrificed, and that the games should be held every hundred years." 9. Livy says the same in Book 136: "In that same year [17 BC], Caesar Augustus held the Secular Games with great pomp, which once was the custom to hold every hundred years, for these games marked the end of a *saeculum.*" On the other hand, the Records of the Council of Fifteen and the edicts of the divine Augustus seem to testify that the games were repeated after 110 years. So Horace in the song which was sung at the Secular Games designated the length of time as:

> *A fixed circle of ten times eleven years*
> *to bring back song and crowded games*

> *three times in the glorious day and as often*
> *in the sweet night.*

10. This disagreement about the times, if the annals of the ancients are unrolled, turns out to have been a matter of uncertainty for quite some time. The first Secular Games were held after the kings were expelled, in the year 245 after the founding of Rome [509 BC] by Valerius Publicola, ‹according to Antias, when Valerius and Spurius Lucretius were consuls›. According to the Records of the Council of Fifteen, it was in the year 298 of Rome [456 BC] when Marcus Valerius and Spurius Verginius were consuls. ‹The second games, according to Antias,› were in year 408 of Rome [346 BC], when M. Valerius Corvus was ‹consul› for the second time along with C. Poetillius, but in the Records of the Council of Fifteen it is written as having occurred in the year of Rome 410 [344 BC], with the consuls ‹C. Marcius Rutilius for the third time and T. Manlius Imperiosus›. The third games, according to both Antias and Livy, were held when P. Claudius Pulcher and L. Iunius Pullus were consuls, ‹in the year 505 [249 BC]; but according to the Records of the Council of Fifteen,› they were held in the year 518 [236 BC], when P. Cornelius Lentulus and C. Licinius Varus were consuls. 11. There are three dates for the fourth Secular Games: Antias, Varro, and Livy say that they were held when L. Marcius Censorinus and Manius Manilius were consuls, in the year 605 after the foundation of Rome [149 BC]. However, Piso the former Censor and Gnaeus Gellius, as well as Cassius Hemina, who were alive at that time, affirm that they were held three years later, when Gnaeus Cornelius Lentulus and Lucius Mummius Achaicus

were consuls, that is, in 608 [146 BC]; while in the Records of the Council of Fifteen they are put under the year 628 [126 BC], with M. Aemilius Lepidus and L. Aurelius Orestes consuls. The fifth Secular Games were held by Caesar Augustus and Agrippa in the consulship of C. Furnius and C. Iunius Silanus in the year 737 [17 BC]. The Emperor Claudius held the sixth games when he was consul for the fourteenth time and L. Vitellius for the third, in 800 [AD 47]. Domitian held the seventh, when he was consul for the fourteenth time along with L. Minucius Rufus, in 841 [AD 88]. The Emperors Septimius Severus and Caracalla held the eighth games, with Cilo and Libo consuls, in 957 [AD 204].

12. From this list one can notice that these games were not established to be repeated either after 100 years or after 110. Further, even if either of these two intervals had been observed in the past, this would not be an argument that one could use to prove that the century was regularly marked off by the Secular Games, especially since there is no record that they were held during the 244 years from the founding of the city to the expulsion of the kings, which is beyond a doubt a period longer than a natural cycle or century. 13. If anyone believes that the *saeculum* is marked by the Secular Games, led only by the origin of the name, he should realize that many things can be called "centennial" (*saeculare*) because most happen only once in a person's lifetime. So in everyday speech we say of many things that are infrequent that they come "once a century."

Although our ancestors were not sure how long a "natural" century was, they had fixed the civil century at 100 years. Piso is our authority. He wrote in Book 7 of *The Annals*: "Rome founded 600 years ago began its seventh century with these consuls, who were also the consuls for the following year: M. Aemilius Lepidus the Younger and C. Popilius for the second time (absent)" [158 BC].

It was not without reason that our ancestors established this number of years. First, because they had seen a number of their fellow citizens live to this age, and then because they wished to imitate the Etruscans in this as in so many other things, who originally had "ages" of 100 years. 14. It is also possible that this came about because, as Varro relates and Dioscorides the astronomer wrote, at Alexandria, those who mummify the dead agree that a human cannot live more than 100 years. The human heart declares the same thing, they say, at least the heart of people who died untouched by wasting disease. For many years they have weighed the hearts of people of all ages and noted the increases and decreases: the heart of a one-year-old weighs about two-tenths of an ounce, a two-year-old's weighs four-tenths of an ounce, and so on, increasing two-tenths of an ounce every year up to age fifty, with a maximum weight of ten ounces. From age fifty onwards, it loses two-tenths of an ounce each year. From this is can be seen that at age 100 the heart has returned to its weight at age one and can extend life no longer.

15. Therefore, since the civil century of the Romans lasts 100 years, we know that your first birthday took place in the tenth century since the founding of Rome, and so does today's birthday. As for how many centuries are allotted to the city of Rome, it is not for me to say, but I will not pass over in silence what I have read in Varro, who says in Book 18 of *The Antiquities* that at Rome there was a certain man named Vettius, not

without power in augury, a great natural talent, and the equal of any scholar in debate. Varro heard him say that if it happened as the Roman historians have recorded, that Romulus saw twelve vultures as an augury when he founded the City, then since the Roman people had passed 120 years unharmed, they would make it to 1,200 years.

18 ⋆ *The Great Year*

1. But enough about the century. Now I shall speak about the Great Year, whose size is as differently observed by various peoples as it is handed down by various authors, so that some have thought that the Great Year consists of two complete years, while others say it consists of many thousands. I will now try to settle what it really is.

2. The ancient states of Greece had noticed that, during the time the sun takes to complete its circuit in its annual course, sometimes twelve and sometimes thirteen new moons arise and that this alternates year by year. They realized that twelve and a half lunar months made up a natural, solar year. Accordingly, they set up their civil years so that by adding an inserted or "intercalary" month, one year had twelve lunar months, the next thirteen. Each year ran separately but the two joined together they called the Great Year. They called this period a *tri-eteris*—that is, a triennium, or period of three years—because the extra month is inserted every third year, even though the circuit takes two years to complete and is really a "biennial." (This, by the way, is why the mysteries celebrated every other year for the god Liber are called *trieteris*— "triennial," by the poets.) 3. Later on when the discrepancy

between the lunar and solar calendars became noticeable, they doubled it to a four-year period, but because the intercalary month came back every fifth year, they called the period "five-years," or a quinquennium. This type of Great Year, composed of four years, seemed more convenient, because they realized that the solar year consisted of 365 days and about one-fourth of a day, which makes one additional whole day in each four years. 4. This is why the Games at Elis for Jupiter of Olympus (the Olympic Games) and the Games at Rome for Jupiter of the Capitoline are celebrated every four years. This period of time, which seems to match up only with the course of the sun and not the moon, was in turn doubled to an eight-year period (again called "nine-years" by the Greeks, because the first year of the cycle returned in Year Nine). 5. Most of Greece considered this cycle to be the real Great Year, because it consisted of a whole number of years and a whole number of lunar months, as ought to be the case in a Great Year. This Great Year consists of 2,922 complete days, ninety-nine complete lunar months, and eight complete years. This eight-year period is commonly believed to have been set up by Eudoxus of Cnidos, but others say that Cleostratus of Tenedos was to first to invent it, and after him there were others who invented their own systems of eight years using various types of additional months, for example Harpalus, Nauteles, Menestratus, and others, including Dositheus, whose book is actually entitled *On the Eight Year System of Eudoxus*. 6. For this reason, in Greece many religious festivals are celebrated at this interval with special ceremony. For example, the Pythian Games at Delphi were originally held every eight years. Next comes the duodecennial, composed of twelve years. 7. This is named the

Chaldean Year, which the astrologers did not base directly on the sun or moon but on other observations, because they say that weather, good and bad harvests, as well as diseases and healthy times go around in this cycle.

8. There are many other Great Years, such as the one named for Meton of Athens, called the *enneadeka-eteris,* composed of nineteen years, with seven additional months, for a total of 6,940 days. There is also the Great Year of Philolaus the Pythagorean, with 59 years and 21 additional months; that of Callippus of Cyzicus with 76 years and 28 months inserted; one from Democritus with 82 years and 28 added months. 9. And finally, Hipparchus, with 304 years, into which 112 additional months are inserted.

The lengths of these Great Years do not agree, because the astronomers do not agree on how much more than 365 days the sun takes in a year and how much less than thirty days the moon takes in a month. 10. The moon has nothing to do with the Great Year of the Egyptians, which in Greek is called the *Kyníkon* (in Latin we call it the "Dog Star Year"), because it starts on the first day of the month, which the Egyptians call the Month of Thoth, on which Sirius the Dog Star rises. Their civil year has exactly 365 days with no additional day. Since they have no leap year, their four-year cycle is about one day shorter than the natural four-year cycle, and so it only returns to the same point, where the start of the two cycles match, every 1,461 years. This is called by some the Heliacal or Solar Year, and by others the Year of God.

11. There is also the Year which Aristotle called the Greatest, rather than merely the Great, which the orbits of the sun, moon, and five planets determine, when they all return to-

gether to the same sign of the zodiac in which they were at the start. This Year has a great winter called the *Cataclysm,* which we call the Deluge, and a summer called the *Ekpyrosis,* that is, the Conflagration of the World, for at these two times the world apparently is either drowned in water or set on fire. Aristarchus thought this took 2,434 solar years; Aretes of Dyrrachium, 5,552; Heraclitus and Linus, 10,800; Dion, 10,884; Orpheus, 120,000; and Cassandrus, 3,600,000 years. Others think it is infinite and will never return.

12. But of all these units for marking time, the Greeks use above all else cycles of four years, which they call "Olympiads." We are currently in the second year of the 254th Olympiad [AD 238].

13. For the Romans, the Great Year was the same as what was called the *lustrum.* It was established by the Etruscan king Servius Tullius that every fifth year a census of the citizens should be held and the lustrum declared over, but the custom was not kept up by the later Romans. 14. Between the first lustrum declared by King Servius Tullius and the last one, which was held by the Emperor Vespasian (consul for the fifth time) and his son Titus Caesar (consul for the third time) [in AD 74], there have been a little less than 650 years, but in all that time the lustrum was held seventy-five times at most, and after that they ceased to be held at all. 15. But on the other hand, the Great Year has recently begun to be observed regularly in the form of the Capitoline Games, which were first set up by Domitian in his twelfth consulship and Servius Cornelius Dolabella's first [AD 86]. And so this year we are celebrating the thirty-ninth Capitoline Games.

Enough has been said about the various Great Years; now is the place for talking about the regular year. 19.1. The natural year is the time it takes the Sun to run through the twelve signs and return to the same place it set out from. 2. The astronomers have not been able to determine with complete certainty how many days this is. Philolaus wrote that the natural year has 364 ½ days; Aphrodisius, 365 ⅛ days; Callippus, 365 [¼] days; Aristarchus of Samos, the same number plus $\frac{1}{1623}$ of a day [365 ¼ + $\frac{1}{1623}$ days]; Meton, 365 $\frac{5}{19}$ days; Oenopides, 365 $\frac{22}{59}$ days; Harpalus, 365 days and 13 hours (the standard hours on an equinox, that is); and our own poet Ennius, 366. 3. Most have thought that it could not be measured accurately or expressed in regular fractions, but they have taken as the closest to the truth the round number of 365 days.

4. When there has been such disagreement among the most learned men, is it any wonder that the various civil years, which were established by different primitive societies each for its own purposes, are different from each other and fail to match the natural year? Even in Egypt, they say that the "year" in the most ancient period lasted only one month, then it was increased to four months by King Ison, and most finally by Arminos to thirteen months and five days. 5. So too in Achaea, the Arcadians are said to have had originally a "year" that lasted three months. This is why they were called *pro-selenes,* not, as some think, because they were created before the moon was in the sky, but because they set up their year before the rest of Greece matched the year to the phases of the moon. 6. Some

write that the Egyptian god Horus founded this three month "year," and therefore spring, summer, autumn, and winter are called the *horai* ("seasons" in Greek), the full year is called *horos,* the Greek historical annals are *horoi* ("years"), and the people who write them are called *horographers.* And so they called a cycle of four little "years" the Big Year, in the same way that four regular years form a quadrennium (the Greek *penta-eteris*). 7. Both the Carians and the Acarnanians had "years" that lasted six months, but the "years" were different, so that in the first "year" the days grew longer (spring and summer), and in the second the days grew shorter (fall and winter). Put together (and so recurring every third little "year"), they formed a big year.

20 ⋆ *The Calendar*

1. But I shall omit those years lost in the darkness of profound antiquity. But even among those years which are of more recent memory and regulated by the course of the sun or moon, there is great variety. It is easy to see this, if one will merely look at the peoples of Italy alone (to say nothing of foreigners). For the people of Ferentinum have one year, the people of Lavinium another, so too the Albans, as well as the Romans and the other peoples. Laws were passed by all of them to try to match their civil years to the one true and natural year with the aid of various additional months. 2. But since it would take too long to explain them all, let us pass directly to the year of the Romans.

Licinius Macer and afterwards Fenestella wrote that the

natural year at Rome was twelve months long from the beginning. But Iunius Gracchanus, Fulvius, Varro, Suetonius, and others are more believable, who think that there were ten months, just as there were at Alba, which is where the Romans came from. 3. These ten months had 304 days as follows: March, 31; April, 30; May, 31; June, 30; Quintilis [July], 31; Sextilis [August] and September, 30; October, 31; November and December, 30. Of these the four longer months were called "full"; the six shorter, "hollow." 4. Afterwards King Numa (as Fulvius says), or Tarquin (so Iunius), created twelve months and a total of 355 days, although the moon in these twelve months was seen to complete only 354 days. The extra one day resulted either from carelessness or, as I believe, from the superstition that holds odd numbers as "full" and luckier. 5. In any case, 51 days were definitely added to the old year. Since these did not make two complete months, one day was taken from each of the six short "hollow" months, and added to these 51 days, making a total of 57, and these were split into two months: January with 29, and February with 28 days. And so all the months started off with an odd or "full" number of days, except for February, which alone was "hollow" and therefore considered unluckier that the rest. 6. Later, when it was decided to add an intercalary month of 22 or 23 days every other year, so that the civil year would equal out to the natural year, it was inserted into the month of February, between the festivals of Terminalia on the 23rd and Refugium on the 24th. They did this for a long time before it was realized that the civil years were a little bit longer than the natural years. The pontifices were entrusted with correcting this error and the additions to the calendar were made according to their calculations. 7. But many pontifices, acting out of hatred or favor, played with the calendar, making it longer or shorter as they liked, so that some enemy might be forced to leave a civic office earlier or a friend might enjoy it longer, or so that some tax collector might make a profit or a loss because of the length of the year. In this way they ruined the very thing that had been handed over to them to correct. 8. Things got so bad that Julius Caesar, when he was pontifex maximus, during his third consulship, which he shared with M. Aemilius Lepidus [46 BC], in order to correct the accumulated errors, had to insert two intercalary months with a total of 67 days between November and December, even though he had already made the usual addition of 23 days in February, adding up to a total of 445 days for that year. At the same time he made sure that the problem would not return in the future, for he removed the additional month from the calendar and made the civil year conform to the course of the sun. 9. He added 10 days to the old 355, dividing them up among the seven months that had 29 days. January, Sextilis [August], and December got two, the others (April, June, September, November) got one. He added these days at the end of each month, so that the religious festivals would not be moved from their usual places in the month. 10. That is why to this day we have seven months with 31 days, but we can recognize the four which were set up in the ancient system by the fact that they have the Nones on the seventh day, but the other three long months and all the short months have them on the fifth.

And to take care of the quarter of a day, which seems left over after the real year is done, Caesar established that after a cycle of four years was completed, one day should be inserted after Terminalia, the 23rd of February, where the old additional month used to be, which we now call Leap Day. 11. Because of the way that Julius Caesar set up this year, beginning with his fourth consulship [45 BC] all the years down to our time have been called "Julian." His system is the best, but the others were also altered to fit the natural year. The ancient systems of years were corrected in the same sort of way, as far as they could be, even our old ten-month calendar, both at Rome and in the rest of Italy and among various peoples. 12. And so when I talk about any particular number of years from now on, you should understand that I mean only natural, solar years.

21 ⋆ *The History of the World*

If the date of the origin of the world had come down to human knowledge, we would take our start from that. 21.1. But as it is, I will now deal with the part of time that Varro calls "Historical." He says there are three periods of time: the first from the origin of man to the first Cataclysm, which because of our ignorance is called the "Uncertain"; the second from the first Cataclysm to the first Olympiad [776 BC], which, because many legends are ascribed to it, he calls the "Mythical"; and the third, from the first Olympiad to our time, which he calls the "Historical," because the events which occurred in it are contained in factual histories. 2. The number of years in the first age, whether it had a beginning or existed forever, obviously cannot be known. The second age is not known for sure, but it is generally believed to have been around 1,600 years long. From the first Cataclysm, often called that of Ogy-

gius, son of Cadmus and King of Thebes, to the reign of Inachus, first King of Argos, was about 400 years. ‹From then
to the Trojan War was about 800 years,› and from then to
the first Olympiad was a little more than 400. The years between the Trojan War and the first Olympiad were the last
of the Mythical period, but because they were the closest to
written memory, some have wished to fix the interval with
greater precision. 3. So Sosibius wrote that it was 395 years
[the Trojan War, then, took place in 1171 BC]; Eratosthenes,
407 [1183 BC]; Timaeus, 417 [1193 BC]; and Aretes, 514 [1290
BC]. Others have different opinions, but their very diversity
shows the uncertainty.

4. When it comes to the third age, the disagreement between authors usually amounted to no more than six or seven
years. 5. But Varro has dispersed even this amount of darkness.
With his usual great intelligence, he used two methods. First,
by comparing the chronologies of different civilizations, and
then by counting back thorough the number of solar eclipses
and the number of years between them, he has dug up the truth
and shown the light, so that it is possible to know not only the
exact number of years, but sometimes even days.

6. Following his calculations, if I am not mistaken, this
year, to which we Romans give the name and title of the consuls, the honorable Pius and Pontianus, is the 1014th since the
first Olympiad (which starts during the summer, when the
Olympic Games are celebrated) and the 991st since the foundation of Rome (the years of the City are numbered starting
on the Festival of the Parilia, Rome's birthday, April 21) [i.e.,
AD 238]. 7. In terms of Julian Years, it is 283 (starting on 1
January, which Julius Caesar made the beginning of the year

which he invented). 8. In the years which are called Augustan, it is 265 (again, starting on 1 January, although in fact it was on 17 January, with the motion made by L. Munatius Plancus, that the Emperor Octavian Caesar, adopted son of the Divine Julius, was first called Augustus by the Senate and people of Rome). This was during his seventh and M. Vipsanius Agrippa's third consulships [27 BC]. 9. But the Egyptians, because they came into the power and jurisdiction of the Roman people two years earlier, count this as the 267th year of the Augustan era.

Just as we do, the Egyptians use different systems for recording the years. One system is named for King Nabonassar, starting at the first year of his reign [747 BC]; this is currently year 986. They also use the Year of Philip, the successor of Alexander the Great, which numbers from Alexander's death [323 BC], and so far adds up to 562. 10. These years always start on the first day of the month the Egyptians call Thoth, which fell this year on 25 June, but 100 years ago (the second consulship of the Emperor Antoninus Pius with Bruttius Praesens at Rome), it was on 20 July, the very day on which Sirius the Dog Star usually rises over the horizon for the first time in Egypt. 11. So it is obvious that we are currently in Year 100 of that Great Year, mentioned above, called the Solar, Canicular, or Year of God. 12. I have noted above the proper starting days for each of these years so that no one will think that they all begin on 1 January or any other single date, for the wishes of their founders differed no less than the opinions of the philosophers. 13. The natural year seemed to some to start at the new sun, that is, the winter solstice; to others, at the summer solstice; to very many, at the vernal equinox; to others, at the autumnal equinox; to a couple, at the rising of the Pleiades; to several, at their setting; to not a few, at the rising of Sirius.

22 ⋆ *Months*

1. Now months. There are two types, natural and civil. 2. There are two types of natural months, named respectively for the sun and the moon. The solar month lasts the amount of time it takes the sun to run through one sign of the zodiac. The lunar month is the space of time between new moons. 3. Civil months are a given number of days which each state observes according to its own institutions, for example, now at Rome, from Kalend [the first day of each month] to Kalend. The natural months are both older and common to all states; the civil were set up later and apply to each individual state. 4. The astronomical months, solar or lunar, are not themselves completely uniform in length nor composed of whole numbers of days. For example, the sun stays in Aquarius for about 29 days; in Pisces, about 30; in Aries, 31; in Gemini, almost 32; and so on, unequally in the other signs. These fractional days in each sign add up to 365 days plus a certain portion not yet determined by the astronomers, and these are divided into twelve months. 5. The moon also creates its own months of about 29 ½ days, but these too are unequal, some longer, some shorter. The months of the various states differ even more in the number of days per month, but each has a whole number of days. 6. So among the people of Alba, March is 36 days

long; May, 22; August, 18; September, 16. Among the people of Tusculum, July has 36 days; October, 32. And for the people of Aricia, October goes on for 39 days.

7. Those who accommodated the civil months to the course of the moon seem to have erred the least amount, for example, most of the cities in Greece, among which every other month lasted thirty days. 8. Our ancestors imitated this when they had a year of 355 days. But the divine Julius Caesar, when he saw that in this system the months did not correspond as they should to the moon, nor did the year correspond to the sun, preferred to correct the year, so that the civil months would correspond to the true solar months, not on an individual basis but taken all together at the end of the year.

9. Fulvius and Iunius are our sources that Romulus gave the names to the ten ancient Roman months, and further that he named the first two after his parents: March from his father, Mars, and April from Aphrodite, that is, Venus, from whom his ancestors were said to have descended. The next two are from the people: May from the *maiores,* the older men; June from the juniors; the rest from their numerical order, Quintilis (July, number five), right to December (number ten).

10. Varro, on the other hand, taught quite brilliantly that the Romans got the names of the months from the Latins, having realized that their sources were older than the City itself. 11. So he believed that March was indeed named for Mars, not because he was the father of Romulus, but because the Latin tribe was warlike. He derived April not from Aphrodite, but from "opening," *aperio,* because almost everything is created then and nature *opens* the doors for birth. 12. May does not come from *maiores,* but takes its name from the goddess

Maia, because in that month, in Rome as well as Latium, the sacrifices for Maia and Mercury were held. June also comes from Juno rather than the "juniors," because in that month special honors are paid to Juno. 13. Quintilis [July], because it was in fifth place in the Latins' calendar; the same for Sextilis to December, according to their number. Finally, January and February were indeed added later, but with names taken from Latium: January took its name from the god Janus, to whom it was dedicated, and February from the old word *februum*. 14. Anything that consecrates or purifies is a *februum*; *februamenta* are purifications, and *febru-are* is to purify and make clean. The same thing, however, is not always said to be a *februum*; for things become *februum*, that is purified, in different ways in different rites. 15. For example, in the month of February, at the Lupercalia, the festival when Rome is purified, they carry around hot salt, which is called *februum*. So the Lupercalia is more properly called *Februatus,* "purified," and therefore the month is called February.

16. Of the twelve months, only two have changed their names. For Quintilis was renamed July, in the fifth consulship of *Julius* Caesar with Marc Antony, in year 2 of the Julian calendar [44 BC]. What had been Sextilis was called August in honor of Augustus Caesar by order of the senate, when C. Marcius Censorinus and C. Asinius Gallus were consuls, in year 20 of the Augustan Era [8 BC]. These names remain to the present time. 17. Afterwards, many emperors changed the names of certain months and called them after themselves, but they either changed them later, or the old names were given back to the months after the emperors' deaths.

1. It remains to say a few things about the day. The day, like the year or the month, is either natural or civil. 2. The natural day is the time from sunrise to sunset; its opposite is night, from sunset to sunrise. The civil day is the name of the time necessary for one complete revolution of the heavens; it therefore contains both the true day (daytime) and night (nighttime). For example, when we say that someone lived for only thirty days, it goes without saying that nights are included. 3. "Day" in this sense is defined in four ways by astronomers and states. The Babylonians established it as from the rising of the sun to the next rising of that same star, but most of the peoples of Umbria say from noon to noon, and the Athenians, from sunset to sunset. The Romans, however, counted the day from midnight to midnight. 4. Our public sacrifices and the auspices taken by the magistrates are proof: if something happened before midnight, it is dated to the day which has passed; if anything happens after midnight and before dawn, it is said to have occurred on the day which followed that night. 5. The same thing is shown by the fact that those who are born in the twenty-four hours between one midnight and the next all have the same birthday.

6. It is well-known that daytime is divided into twelve hours and so is the night. However, this custom was observed at Rome, I believe, only after the invention of the sundial. It is difficult to find out which was the most ancient sundial. Some say the first one was put up next to the Temple of Quirinus, others on the Capitoline, some next to the Temple of Diana on the Aventine. 7. However, it is agreed that there was no

sundial in the Forum before the one which Manius Valerius carried off from Sicily and placed on a column near the Rostra. But since it was calibrated for the latitude of Sicily, it did not work for the hours at Rome, so L. Philippus, when he was censor, set up another next to it. Then a little bit later, P. Cornelius Scipio Nasica made a water clock, which was also called the "sundial" because of the usual way of telling the hours by the sun. 8. It is likely that the word "hour" was not used at Rome for at least 300 years. You will not find "hours" mentioned in our oldest laws, The Laws of the Twelve Tables (as they are in later laws), but they do use the phrase *ante meridiem,* "before noon," "before the half-day," because noon divided the day into two halves. 9. Others divided the day into four parts, and the night also. Military language shows something similar, when they talk about first, second, third, and fourth "watches."

24 ⋆ *Hours*

1. There are many other divisions of the day and night, calculated in various ways, and distinguished by individual names which are found written in the old poets. I'll set them all out in proper order, beginning from midnight (*nox media*), which is both the end and the beginning of the Roman day. The next period is called "after midnight" (*de media nocte*). 2. There follows "cock-crow" (*gallicinium*), when the roosters begin to sing; then "silence" (*conticinium*), when they fall silent; then "predawn" (*ante lucem*) and "break of day" (*diluculum*), when there is light even though the sun has not yet risen.

3. There is a second kind of daybreak called "morning"

(*mane*), when light from the risen sun is seen; after this, "forenoon" (*ad meridiem*); then "noon" (*meridies*), which is the word for the middle of the day; next, "afternoon" (*de meridie*); then "the final hour" (*suprema*), though many think that the final hour is after the sun sets, because in the Twelve Tables it is written: "Sunset shall be the final time of the day." But later, M. Plaetorius, when he was tribune, passed a plebiscite, in which it was written: "The current praetor of the city, and any later ones, shall have two lictors with him, and let him give judgment among the citizens up to the final hour, that is, sunset." 4. After "final hour" comes *vesper,* or "evening," since it occurs before the rising of Vesper, the Evening Star, which Plautus calls Vesperugo, Ennius called Vesper, and Virgil called Hesperos. 5. Then, *crepusculum,* or "twilight," possibly so called because uncertain things are called *creper,* and it is uncertain whether the time is day or night.

6. After that follows the time we call "with the lights lit" (*luminibus accensis*), which the ancients called "first torch" (*prima face*); then "bedtime" (*concubium*), time for bed; then the "untimely" hour (*intempesta*), deep night, when it is an unlucky time to do anything; then "just before midnight" (*ad mediam noctem*); and finally midnight again.

All the manuscripts of Censorinus stop here. Since he promised to give the exact day of his friend's birthday (chapter 16.1), we know a little has been lost. We are perhaps missing the last five chapters. The praise of Quintus Caerellius is the high point of the book. It comes in chapter 15, with fourteen

chapters leading up to it. It is possible that five chapters were intended to follow, giving a total of twenty-nine, the number of days in a lunar month. In the last chapters, Censorinus would have undoubtedly told his friend's birthday and cast his horoscope. — Trans.

◦ GLOSSARY ◦

Academy. The site of the school of philosophy founded by Plato. Named for the grove of Academus just outside Athens.

Acarnanians. People of a mountainous and primitive region of Greece.

Achaea. Ancient area of southern Greece, containing Arcadia.

Aemilius, Marcus. Roman consul in 158 BC.

Aemilius Lepidus, Marcus. Roman consul in 126 BC.

Aemilius Lepidus, Marcus. Roman consul in 46 BC.

Agrippa (Marcus Vipsanius). Around 64–12 BC. Right-hand man to Emperor Augustus.

Alba (Alba Longa). Ancient town in Italy. In myth it was founded by Aeneas's son Ascanius. Many of the customs of Rome were said to come from Alba.

Alcmaeon (of Croton, in southern Italy). Fifth century BC. Pre-Socratic, Pythagorean philosopher, who wrote on the nature of humankind.

Anaxagoras. Around 500–428 BC. Pre-Socratic philosopher, who envisioned a cosmos created out of an original mixture of all things by Mind.

Anaximander (of Miletus, in Turkey). Died around 547 BC. First philosopher to write a book called *On Nature.* He saw a universe where all things are separated out of an original unity, called the Boundless, and return to it in cosmic cycles.

Antias (Valerius Antias). First century BC Roman historian.

Antoninus Pius. Roman emperor, AD 138–61.

Antony, Marc. 83–30 BC. Lover of Cleopatra and opponent of the future emperor Augustus.

Aphrodisius. Greek astronomer otherwise unknown.

Archytas (of Tarentum). Flourished around 400–350 BC. Pythagorean philosopher and mathematician.

Arcadia. Mountainous and archaic region of central Greece.

Aretes (of Dyrrachium). Greek Astronomer of unknown date.

Arganthonion. Legendary king of Tartessus, in southern Spain. Herodotus *The Histories* 1.163 tells his story.

Aricia. Ancient city near Rome.

Aristarchus (of Samos). Observed the summer solstice of 280 BC. Greek astronomer; the first to propose a heliocentric system.

Aristotle (of Stagira in Chalcidice, in modern Macedonia). 384–322 BC. Famous Greek philosopher and tutor to Alexander the Great.

Aristoxenus. Born c. 370 BC. Philosopher and famous scholar of music.

Arminos. Legendary king of Egypt.

Asclepiades (of Bythinia). First century BC. Greek doctor.

Asinius Gallus, Gaius. Roman consul in 8 BC.

Augustus. 63 BC–14 AD. The first Roman emperor.

Aurelius Orestes, Lucius. Roman consul in 126 BC.

Aventine. Hill in Rome.

Berosos. Around 290 BC. Babylonian scholar and historian.

Boeotia. Region of northern Greece.

Bruttius Praesens. Roman consul in AD 138.

Cadmus. Legendary founder of Thebes in Boeotia.

Caerellius, Quintus. Censorinus's great friend, to whom he gave *The Birthday Book* in AD 238, when he had passed his forty-ninth year. We know nothing about him apart from the portrait given here of a provincial who rose to the Roman knighthood.

Callippus (of Cyzicus). Around 330 BC. Greek astronomer. Pupil of Eudoxus and friend of Aristotle.

Capitoline. Most important hill in Rome, site of the Temple of Jupiter.

Caracalla. Roman emperor, AD 198–217.

Carians. Ancient Anatolian people of southwestern Turkey.

Carneades. 214–129 BC. Greek philosopher. Head of the Academy, the school of philosophy founded by Plato. Founder of the New Academy.

Cassandrus. Greek astronomer of unknown date.

Cassius Hemina. Around 146 BC. One of the earliest Roman historians.

Chaldeans. People of ancient Mesopotamia, famed for their knowledge of astrology.

Cilo and *Libo.* Roman consuls in AD 204.

Claudius. Roman emperor, 41–54 AD.

Claudius Pulcher, Publius. Roman consul in 249 BC.

Cleanthes. 331–232 BC. Greek philosopher and successor to Zeno as head of the Stoic school.

Cleostratus (of Tenedos). Sixth century BC. Greek astronomer.

Colchis. Area in the Black Sea where Jason sailed to find the Golden Fleece.

Collian Gate. Northern gate in the old walls of Rome.

Consul. Chief magistrate at Rome. Roman years were named after the two presiding consuls.

Cornelius Dolabella, Servius. Roman consul in AD 86.

Cornelius Lentulus, Gnaeus. Roman consul in 146 BC.

Cornelius Lentulus, Publius. Roman consul in 236 BC.

Cornelius Scipio Nasica (Corculum), Publius. Roman consul in 162 and 155 BC; censor in 159 BC. Set up a water clock in Rome.

Delos. Aegean island, birthplace of Apollo.

Delphi. Home of Apollo's oracle in northern Greece.

Democritus (of Abdera). Fifth century BC. Greek philosopher, famous for being the first to think the world was composed of individual particles, which he called "atoms."

Deucalion and *Pyrrha.* The Ancient Greek Noah and his wife. After the Flood, they were ordered to repopulate the world by "throwing the bones of their Mother behind them." They threw stones from which sprang new humans.

Dicaearchus (of Messenia). Around 320–300 BC. Pupil of Aristotle. He wrote many books on literature, politics, geography, and history.

Diocles (of Carystus). Fourth century BC. Greek doctor, second in fame only to Hippocrates.

Diogenes (of Apollonia). Late fifth century BC. He held a theory of infinite worlds in an infinite void.

Diogenes (the Cynic). Around 412–321 BC. Founder of the Cynic school of philosophy. He is famous for his outrageous lifestyle and his search (with a lamp) for an honest man.

Dion (of Naples). Greek astronomer of unknown date.

Dionysius (of Heraclea). Around 328–248 BC. Greek philosopher and pupil of Zeno.

Dioscorides. Greek astrologer of uncertain date.

Domitian. Roman emperor, AD 81–96.

Dorylaus. Otherwise unknown.

Dositheus. Around 230 BC. Greek astronomer and mathematician. Friend of Archimedes.

Elis. City in charge of the Olympic Games.

Empedocles. Around 492–432 BC. Pre-Socratic poet and philosopher who wrote of a comic cycle caused by the two forces Love and Strife.

Ennius. 239–169 BC. One of the earliest Roman poets.

ephebe (*ep-* "at" + *hebe* "youth"). The term for Greek male adolescents. At Athens the term usually meant young men between eighteen and twenty on special military service.

Ephorus. Around 405–330 BC. Greek historian.

Epicharmus. First quarter of fifth century BC. Greek comic poet.

Epicurus. 341–270 BC. Greek philosopher, major exponent of the atomic theory of the universe (see *Democritus*). He held that ethical action should be guided by pleasure.

Epigenes (of Byzantium). Second century BC. Greek/Chaldean astrologer.

Equestrians. The "knights," or second highest order of Roman nobility, ranking just after senators.

Eratosthenes. Around 285–194 BC. Greek literary scholar, mathematician, and astronomer who measured the circumference of the earth with remarkable accuracy.

Erichthonius. Legendary king of Athens. Vulcan (the Greek god Hephaestus) tried to rape Athena, but he only managed to ejaculate on her clothing. Athena, in disgust, wiped off the drops, which fell to earth. From these sprang Erichthonius.

Esquiline Gate. Eastern gate in the old city wall of Rome.

Etruscans. Ancient non-Indo-European people of Italy, whose language remains in part undeciphered, famed for skill in foretelling the future.

Euclides (of Megara). Around 450–380 BC. Greek philosopher and pupil of Socrates.

Eudoxus (of Cnidos). Around 390–340 BC. Greek mathematician and astronomer.

Euenor. Later part of fourth century BC. Greek doctor.

Euryphon (of Cnidus). Fifth century BC. Greek doctor.

Fenestella. 52 BC–AD 19. Roman scholar and historian.

Ferentinum. Ancient Italian city near Rome.

Fulvius (Marcus Fulvius Nobilior). Roman consul in 189 BC. A great general and patron of Ennius.

Furnius, Gaius. Roman consul in 17 BC.

Gellius, Gnaeus. Later second century BC. Roman historian.

Gorgias (of Leontini). Around 485–380 BC. Greek orator.

Granius Flaccus. Second half of first century BC. Roman grammarian and scholar who wrote on ancient Roman religion.

Harpalus. Fifth century BC. Greek astronomer.

Heraclitus. Around 500 BC. Greek philosopher who visualized a universe in constant change, but held in balance like a strung bow.

Herodicus. Probably Herodicus of Babylon, second century BC. Greek scholar.

Herodotus. Around 480–420 BC. Called the "Father of History" for his brilliant story of the Persian Wars.

Herophilus. Around 330–260 BC. Alexandrian physician and anatomist. One of the most brilliant doctors of the ancient world.

Hipparchus. Second half of second century BC. Greek astronomer.

Hippocrates (of Cos). Late fifth century BC. Most famous doctor of antiquity.

Hippon (of Metapontum or Samos). Fifth century BC. Greek philosopher.

Horace. 65–8 BC. The greatest Roman lyric poet.

Ides. The Roman calendar counted down to three important days in each month: the Kalends (whence our word "calendar"), always the first day; the Ides (as in "the Ides of March"), usually the thirteenth day; and the Nones, nine days before the Ides, and so usually the fifth day. However, the dates of the Ides and Nones varied, depending on the month; for the reason, see chapter 20.10.

Inachus. Mythical first King of Argos.

Isocrates. 436–338 BC. Greek orator.

Ison. Legendary King of Egypt.

Iunius Gracchanus. Around 120 BC. Roman scholar.

Iunius Pullus, Lucius. Roman consul in 249 BC.

Iunius Silanus, C. Roman consul in 17 BC.

Julius Caesar. 100–44 BC. Roman general and writer. His calendar remained in effect until the reforms of Pope Gregory XIII (not adopted in England until 1752). The Julian calendar is still officially used by the Greek and Russian Orthodox Churches.

Kalends. See *Ides.*

Lar. The *lares familares* (plural) were the small domestic gods of the Romans, worshiped with simple offerings at household shrines.

Lavinium. Ancient city near Rome, where Aeneas first landed.

Lepidus, Marcus, the Younger. Roman consul in 158 BC.

Licinius Macer. Died in 66 BC. Roman historian.

Licinius Varus, Gaius. Roman consul in 236 BC.

Linus. Mythical teacher of Orpheus.

Livy. 59 BC–AD 17. Roman historian.

Lucilius. Around 180–101 BC. Roman satiric poet.

Lucretius. Around 94–55 BC. Roman poet. Author of *De Rerum Natura (On the Nature of Things)*, an epic poem on the universe and the philosophy of Epicurus.

Manilius, Manius. Roman consul in 149 BC.

Manlius Imperiosus, Titus. Roman consul in 344 BC.

Marcius Censorinus, Gaius. Roman consul in 8 BC. Perhaps an ancestor of Censorinus.

Marcius Censorinus, Lucius. Roman consul in 149 BC. Perhaps an ancestor of Censorinus.

Marcius Rutilius, Gaius. Roman consul for the third time in 344 BC.

Menestratus. Greek astronomer of uncertain date.

Meton (of Athens). Dated by his having observed the summer solstice of 432 BC. Greek astronomer.

Minerva. Roman form of Athena, goddess of Wisdom.

Minucius Rufus, Lucius. Roman consul in AD 88.

Mummius Achaicus, Lucius. Roman consul in 146 BC.

Munatius Plancus, Lucius. Consul in 43 BC. Served under Julius Caesar. First to make the motion in the senate to give Augustus his title.

Nabonnasar (Nabu-nasir). King of Babylon 747–732 BC.

Nauteles. Greek astronomer of uncertain date.

Nones. See *Ides.*

Numa. Legendary Roman king and lawgiver.

Ocellus (of Lucania). Late fifth century BC. Pre-Socratic philosopher and follower of Pythagoras.

Oenopides. Late fifth century BC. Pre-Socratic philosopher.

Ogyges. Mythological son of Cadmus, King of Thebes.

Orpheus. Mythological poet and son of Apollo. Many mystical and philosophical works were attributed to him.

Parmenides (of Velia). Fifth century BC. Pre-Socratic philosopher and poet.

Peripatetic. The school of philosophy founded by Aristotle, who taught in the Lyceum, a sanctuary of Apollo and gymnasium outside Athens, with pleasant walks (*peripatoi*) where one could discuss philosophy.

Persius. AD 34–62. Roman satirical poet.

Philip (Arridaeus). Half brother and successor of Alexander the Great. Ruled from 323–317 BC.

Philippus, L. As censor in 164 BC, set up a sundial in the Roman forum.

Philolaus. Around 470–390 BC. First Pythagorean to write down the teachings of the school.

Piso (Lucius Calpurnius Piso Frugi), also called "Piso the former Censor." Consul in 133 BC. Roman politician and historian.

Pius and *Pontianus.* Roman consuls when Censorinus wrote, in AD 238.

Plaetorius, Marcus. Tribune of the people around 242 BC.

Plato. Around 429–347 BC. Greek philosopher.

Plautus. Wrote around 205–184 BC. Roman comic playwright.

Poetillius, Gaius. Roman consul in 346 BC.

Pomilius, Gaius. Roman consul for the second time in 158 BC.

Pontifices (pontiffs). The chief religious officers of Rome. The head of the college was the pontifex maximus, a title inherited by the pope.

Prometheus. A Titan and friend to mankind. Prometheus tricked the gods into accepting only the bones and fat of the sacrifice. Zeus in turn took fire away from humans, but Prometheus stole it back. In punishment, Zeus tied him to a rock where an eagle gnawed at his liver, which grew back every night. Hercules eventually rescued him.

Pythagoras (of Samos). Late sixth century BC. Greek philosopher who discovered the Pythagorean theorem. He believed in the transmigration of souls and that the universe was governed by numbers.

Romulus. Legendary founder of Rome. A contest between him and his brother Remus was decided when Romulus saw twelve vultures and Remus only six.

Septimius Severus. Roman emperor, AD 193–211.

Servius Tullius. Sixth king of Rome, traditionally 578–535 BC.

Sibylline books. Books of prophecy consulted by the Roman senate in times of crisis.

Socrates. 469–399 BC. Athenian philosopher.

Solon. Leader (*archon*) of Athens in 594 BC. Athenian lawgiver and poet.

Sosibius. Probably mid-third century BC. Spartan historian.

Staseas. First Peripatetic philosopher to settle in Rome (around 92 BC).

Straton. Third head of the Peripatetic school of philosophy, around 287–269 BC.

Suetonius. Born around AD 70. Roman historian.

Tages. In Etruscan mythology, a divine child who possessed oracular powers.

Tarentine Games. Mysterious public games supposedly named for a shrine of Persephone in Rome called the Tarentum or Terentum.

Tarquin. Last king of Rome, traditionally 534–510 BC. Expelled from Rome for the rape of Lucretia.

Tarquinia. Main city of the Etruscans, north of Rome.

Terence. Around 190–159 BC. Roman comic playwright.

Theano. Daughter of Pythagoras, and one of the first women philosophers. Many later works were attributed to her.

Thebes. City in northern Greece.

Theophrastus. 372–287 BC. Successor to Aristotle as head of the Academy.

Thessaly. Area of northern Greece.

Thoth. Egyptian god of wisdom, writing, and prophecy.

Timaeus. Around 350–260 BC. Greek historian, whose work survives only in fragments.

Titus. Roman emperor, AD 79–81.

Tusculum. Small town southeast of Rome.

Umbria. Ancient area of northeastern Italy.

Valerius, Marcus. Roman consul in 456 BC.

Valerius (Maximus Messalla), Manius. Roman consul in 263 BC. Set up first sundial in the Roman Forum.

Valerius Corvus, Marcus. Roman consul for the second time in 346 BC.

Valerius Publicola. Semi-legendary consul (509, 508, 507, 504 BC) of early Rome.

Varro, Marcus Terentius. 116–27 BC. Great Roman scholar.

Virgil. 70–19 BC. Greatest Roman poet, author of the *Aeneid.*

Verginius, Spurius. Roman consul in 456 BC.

Vespasian. Roman emperor, AD 69–79.

Vettius. Astrologer and prophet mentioned by Censorinus.

Vitellius, Lucius. Roman consul for the third time in AD 47.

Xenocrates. Pupil of Plato and head of the Academy from 339–314 BC.

Xenophanes (of Colophon). Around 570–500 BC. Skeptical philosopher and poet.

Xenophon. Around 428–354 BC. Athenian general, writer, and pupil of Socrates.

Zeno (of Citium). 335–263 BC. Founder of the Stoic school of philosophy.

NOTES

Note numbers refer to the numbered sections in each chapter.

CHAPTER I: *Happy Birthday*

2. *"the indifferents"*: See Seneca, *Letters* 82.10; Cicero, *De Finibus* 3.50–51. For the Stoic philosophers, virtue is the only good, vice the only evil; everything else is "indifferent," although some indifferents—like health and wealth—are "preferred" and others—like sickness and poverty—are "dispreferred." For an introduction, see *The Cambridge Companion to the Stoics,* ed. Brad Inwood (Cambridge: Cambridge University Press, 2003), esp. 14, 241, 263–64, 282, 287–90.

3. *As the comic poet Terence wrote:* The quotation comes from his play *The Self-Tormenter,* 195–96.

4. *Xenophon: Memorabilia* 1.6.10.

5. *Therefore, since you do not lack precious gifts:* Censorinus paraphrases the opening of a poem by Horace *Odes* 4.8, which praises another Censorinus, perhaps an ancestor.

take it for what it's worth: Cf. Catullus 1.8.

7. *"A pig tries to teach Minerva"*: Cicero *Letters to His Friends* 9.18.3; *Academica* 1.18; and compare Theocritus 5.23.

9. *Since they believed that food:* This description of ancient religion draws on the lost works of M. Terentius Varro, whom Censorinus cites next.

10. *libation:* For the custom of "first fruits," cf. Pliny *Natural History* 18.8; Tibullus 1.1.14; Ovid *Fasti* 2.520.

let their hair grow: Cf. Euripides *Bacchae* 494; Virgil *Aeneid* 7.391.

CHAPTER 2: *How to Honor the Genius of the Birthday*

1. *Persius: Satires* 2.1. White stones were used to mark auspicious days on calendars.

2. *unmixed wine:* The Greeks and Romans normally drank their wine mixed with water. For pure wine to the Genius, cf. Tibullus 1.7.50, 2.2.8; Ovid *Tristia* 5.5.12.

Varro, Atticus: A lost work.

3. *Also, on the island of Delos:* The bloodless altar on Delos was famous: Macrobius *Saturnalia* 3.6.2–5, citing Varro's lost *De liberis educandis* (On raising children); Servius on Virgil *Aeneid* 3.85; see also Diogenes Laertius 8.13 (citing Aristotle's lost *Constitution of the Delians*); Cicero *On the Nature of the Gods* 3.88.

CHAPTER 3: *What Is the Spirit of the Birthday?*

1. *A Genius is a god:* This passage is also adapted from Varro; see Augustine *City of God* 7.13. Cf. Seneca *Letters* 110.1. The etymologies are correct: Gen-ius shares the same root as gen-eration, etc. Cf. Festus 84 (Lindsay).

2. *Formulas for Invoking the Gods:* Another lost work. Cf. Servius on *Georgics* 1.21 on these books (citing Varro).

Lar: Plural *lares,* familiar spirits who protected households and crossroads. There are inscriptions to the Lares and the Genius: *CIL* 2.1980, 10.1235.

3. *Many believed that two Geniuses should be worshipped, at least in married households:* The woman's birthday spirit was called her "Juno," so the husband would have his Genius, the wife her Juno. See Seneca *Letters* 110.1; Pliny *Natural History* 2.16.

Euclides of Megara . . . said that a double Genius has been appointed for each of us:

One encourages us to good, the other leads us to evil. Cf. the summary (without name) in Servius on *Aeneid* 6.743, and cf. Plutarch *Moralia* 474b, citing Menander (550–51 Koch) for one daimon and Empedocles (31 B 122 DK) for pairs. For two different sleeps from Euclides, cf. Stobaeus 3.6.63.

Book 16 of Lucilius's Satires: Preserved only in quotations. This passage is lost.

4. *glory, and protection:* An allusion to Horace *Odes* 1.1.2 on his patron Maecenas.

CHAPTER 4: *Seed and Conception*

See W. K. C. Guthrie, *In the Beginning: Some Greek Views on the Origins of Life and the Early State of Man* (Ithaca, N.Y.: Cornell University Press, 1957).

3. *The authorities for the first opinion:* Cf. Varro *On Agriculture* 2.1.3; Augustine *City of God* 12.10.

Plato: Laws 6.781e.

Aristotle: Esp. *Generation of Animals* 3.11 (762b–63a2).

Theophrastus: Summarized by Philo of Alexandria (Philo Judaeus) *On the Eternity of the World* (*De aeternitate mundi*), 117–50, esp. 130. The other authors are fragmentary and Censorinus's quotation is often the only source.

Are birds or eggs created first: For a lengthy discussion of the chicken or the egg, see Macrobius *Saturnalia* 7.16.1–14; also Plutarch *Questiones Conviviales* 2.3 (*Moralia* 636f–37d).

4. *Instead there is a kind of cycle:* A view associated especially with Empedocles. For an accessible account, see Simon Trepanier, *Empedocles: An Interpretation* (New York: Routledge, 2004). For the other early philosophers mentioned by Censorinus, see G. S. Kirk, J. E. Raven, and M. Schofield, *The Presocratic Philosophers*, 2nd ed. (Cambridge: Cambridge University Press, 1983). There are excellent translations and introductions in Robin Waterfield, *The First Philosophers: The Presocratics and Sophists* (Oxford: Oxford University Press, 2000) and Jonathan Barnes, *Early Greek Philosophy*, 2nd rev. ed. (London: Penguin, 2001).

5. *but they have held very different opinions about it:* The text is uncertain.

6. *Prometheus:* For the story, see Horace *Odes* 1.16.13–16; Propertius 3.5.6; Ovid *Metamorphoses* 1.83; Aristophanes *Birds* 686; Pausanias 10.4.4.

Deucalion and *Pyrrha:* For the myth, see Ovid *Metamorphoses* 1.313–415; also Pindar *Olympians* 9.43–46; cf. Plato *Timaeus* 22a; *Critias* 112a; Virgil *Georgics* 1.61–63.

7. *Anaximander:* Kirk-Raven-Schofield, *The Presocratic Philosophers,* 140–42. *Empedocles:* Kirk-Raven-Schofield, *The Presocratic Philosophers,* 302–5. *which Lucretius praised: On the Nature of Things* 1.733.

9. *Epicurus:* Cf. Lucretius 5.795–813.

11. *autochthonous:* For the Athenians as aboriginal, see Herodotus 7.161.3; Thucydides 1.2.5, 2.36.1; Plato *Menexenus* 237b; Isocrates 4.24, 8.49, 12.124–25; Demosthenes 19.261 (also Arcadians). For Arcadians, see Herodotus 8.73.1. No one else seems to claim the Thessalians as autochthonous.

"Nymphs and native-born Satyrs": Virgil *Aeneid* 8.314.

12. *seed of Vulcan:* Vulcan (the Greek god Hephaestus) tried to rape Athena, but he only managed to ejaculate on her clothing. Athena, in disgust, wiped off the drops, which fell to earth. From these sprang King Erichthonius. See Apollodorus *Library of Greek Mythology* 3.14.6.

"Sown Men": For the myth, see Apollonius Rhodius 3.1320–1407; Apollodorus *Library of Greek Mythology* 1.9.23; Ovid *Metamorphoses* 7.120–44; Valerius Flaccus 7.607–43; Pausanius 9.10.1.

13. *Tages:* Cicero *On Divination* 2.50; Columella 10.344–47; Lucan 1.635; Macrobius *Saturnalia* 5.19.2; Festus 492 (Lindsay).

Lucumones: Etruscan for "king," according to Servius on *Aeneid* 2.278. 8.65, 8.475 (cf. 10.202); cf. Livy 1.34.

CHAPTER 5: *Pregnancy*

For Greek views about fetal development, see Hippocrates, "Seed" and "The Nature of the Child" in *Hippocratic Writings,* ed. G. E. R. Lloyd (Harmondsworth: Penguin, 1978), 317–46. There is a selection in *Women's Life in Greece and Rome: A Sourcebook in Translation,* ed. Mary R. Lefkowitz and Maureen B. Fant (Baltimore: Johns Hopkins University Press, 1992), 241–

42. See also Soranus 1.57–58, in *Soranus' Gynecology,* trans. Owsei Temkin (Baltimore: John Hopkins Press, 1956), 58–61; Galen, "The Construction of the Embryo," in *Galen: Selected Works,* trans. P. N. Singer (Oxford: Oxford University Press, 1997), 177–289. For modern summaries (covering the authorities cited by Censorinus), see G. E. R. Lloyd, *Science, Folklore, and Ideology* (Cambridge: Cambridge University Press, 1983), 58–111; Lesley Dean-Jones, *Women's Bodies in Classical Greek Science* (Oxford: Oxford University Press, 1994), 148–224.

2. *where human seed comes from, etc.:* A summary of the opinions of each of the philosophers whom Censorinus cites in chapters 5 and 6, together with some sources and ancient testimonia (other than Censorinus), may be helpful.

Alcmaeon: 5.2–5.3, against Hippon; 5.4, female seed; 5.6, we cannot tell what forms first; 6.4, sex determined by amount of seed. Barnes, *Early Greek Philosophy,* 36–39. Pseudo-Plutarch (Aëtius) *Opinions of the Philosophers* (*Placita*) 5.3 (*Moralia* 905a), 5.17 (907e): Alcmaeon says the head forms first.

Anaxagoras: 5.2–5.3, against Hippon; 5.4, female seed; 6.1, brain forms first; 6.2, ethereal heat in seed; 6.3, nourished through umbilical cord; 6.6, male from right, female from left; 6.8, children resemble whichever parent supplies the most seed. Barnes, *Early Greek Philosophy,* 185–98; Kirk-Raven-Schofield, *The Presocratic Philosophers,* 352–84; Waterfield, *The First Philosophers,* 116–32; Aristotle *Generation of Animals* 763b30–35; Pseudo-Plutarch (Aëtius) *Opinions of the Philosophers* (*Placita*) 5.7 (*Moralia* 905e).

Aristotle: 6.1, follows Empedocles, heart first; 6.2, formed by nature (an oversimplification). Heart first: *Generation of Animals* 734a24, 735a25, 740a4; *Parts of Animals* 665a33–34 (heart and liver). On the process, see *Generation of Animals* esp. 734a17–735a27, 736a25–737a8, 740b35–41a3. Pseudo-Plutarch (Aëtius) *Opinions of the Philosophers* (*Placita*) 5.17 (*Moralia* 907e) claims that Aristotle said the loins form first.

Democritus: 5.2–5.3, against Hippon; 6.1, belly and head form first, 6.5, sex determined by which seed takes hold first. Barnes, *Early Greek Philosophy,* 203–53; Kirk-Raven-Schofield, *The Presocratic Philosophers,* 402–33; Waterfield, *The First Philosophers,* 164–93; Aristotle *Generation of Animals* 764a6–

11, cf. 740a13; Plutarch *On Affection for Offspring* 3 (*Moralia* 495e); Pseudo-Plutarch (Aëtius) *Opinions of the Philosophers* (*Placita*) 5.3 (*Moralia* 905a), 5.5 (905c), 5.7 (905f).

Diogenes: 5.4, male seed only; 6.1, first flesh, then bones, nerves, etc.; 6.3, nourished through cotyledon. Barnes, *Early Greek Philosophy*, 254–60; Kirk-Raven-Schofield, *The Presocratic Philosophers*, 434–52; Waterfield, *First Philosophers*, 194–202; Aristophanes of Byzantium *Epitome of History of Animals* 1.78.

Empedocles: 5.4, female seed; 6.1, heart forms first; 6.6, male from right, female from left; 6.7, temperature of seed of each parent determines offspring's sex and visage. Barnes, *Early Greek Philosophy*, 111–61; Kirk-Raven-Schofield, *The Presocratic Philosophers*, 280–321; Waterfield, *The First Philosophers*, 133–63; Aristotle *Generation of Animals* 764a1–7; Pseudo-Plutarch (Aëtius) *Opinions of the Philosophers* (*Placita*) 5.7 (*Moralia* 905d), 5.10 (906b), 5.11 (906d), 5.12 (906e).

Epicurus: 5.4, female seed; 6.2, formed by nature; 6.10, excess seed splits into twins, temperature determines sex. Pseudo-Plutarch (Aëtius) *Opinions of the Philosophers* (*Placita*) 5.3 (*Moralia* 905a), 5.5 (905c).

Hippon: 5.2, seed comes from marrow; 5.4, male seed only; 6.1, head first to form; 6.3, nourished through cotyledon; 6.4, male from thick seed, female from thin seed; 6.9, excess seed makes twins. See Barnes, *Early Greek Philosophy*, 183–84. His strange "experiment" seems to be recorded only here. Pseudo-Plutarch (Aëtius) *Opinions of the Philosophers* (*Placita*) 5.5 (*Moralia* 905c), 5.7 (905e, f) (where he seems to be confused with Hipponax).

Parmenides: 5.2, seed comes from both right and left part of the body; 5.4, female seed; 5.4, sex determined by competition between seeds; 6.8, right seed resembles father, left seed resembles mother. Kirk-Raven-Schofield, *The Presocratic Philosophers*, 259–60; Waterfield, *The First Philosophers*, 65; Barnes, *Early Greek Philosophy*, 89–90; Aristotle *Generation of Animals* 763b30; Galen *Commentary on Hippocrates Epidemics* 6.48 (17A.1002 Kühn); Pseudo-Plutarch (Aëtius) *Opinions of the Philosophers* (*Placita*) 5.7 (*Moralia* 905e), 5.11 (906d); Caelius Aurelianus *On Chronic Diseases* 4.9.

Stoics: 5.4, male seed only; 6.2, infant formed as a whole, spirit within seed. Zeno or Stoics in general cited in Pseudo-Plutarch (Aëtius) *Opinions of the Philosophers (Placita)* 5.5 (*Moralia* 905c), 5.11 (906d), 5.17 (907e); Pseudo-Galen *History of Philosophy* 109 (19.322 Kühn = H. Diels, *Doxographi Graeci* [Berlin: Reimer, 1879; repr. De Gruyter, 1965], 640); Diogenes Laertius 7.159. Sources collected in *SVF* 129 = J. von Arnim, *Stoicorum veterum fragmenta*, vol. 1. (Leipzig: Teubner, 1905; repr. Stuttgart, 1968).

2. *Parmenides:* Censorinus is really speaking about Parmenides' theories about the origins of male and female. See above.

4. *seed of only the father:* A lively debate in antiquity and one reflected in the resolution of Aeschylus's *Oresteia.* It was not fully settled until Karl Ernst von Baer's discovery of the mammalian and human ovum in 1827 (*De Ovi Mammalium et Hominis genesi* [On the Mammalian Egg and the Origin of Man]). For the range of opinions on the question of whether women produce seed, see Pseudo-Plutarch (Aëtius) *Opinions of the Philosophers (Placita)* 5.5 (*Moralia* 905b–c): in favor, Pythagoras, Epicurus, and Democritus; against, Aristottle and Zeno, with Hippon holding that women emit seed, but it does not contribute to conception (contrary to Censorinus's summary).

CHAPTER 6: *The Fetus*

See also the bibliography and list of opinions in chapter 5.

5.5: Note that the traditional numeration occasionally misdivides sections; so too at chapters 17 (16.9), 19 (18.15), and 21 (20.12).

6.3. *a projection in the womb:* Called a *cotyledon,* which is imaged as something analogous to a nipple on the breast. See Hippocrates *Flesh* 6 (8.592.11–594.4 Littré = 192.22–193.7 Joly). The same belief is attributed to Democritus and Epicurus by Pseudo-Plutarch (Aëtius) *Opinions of the Philosophers (Placita)* 5.16 (*Moralia* 907d–e), and to Diogenes of Apollonia by Aristophanes of Byzantium *Epitome of the History of Animals* 1.78 (64 A 25 DK), though Censorinus says nothing. It is also attributed to Diocles of Carystus (a contemporary of Aristotle) by Soranus 1.14 (10.14–22 Ilberg = A.4.120–30 BGM = Diocles 23c = 27 Wellmann; cf. Oribasius 24.25). Aristotle (*Generation of Animals* 746a19) refutes certain (unnamed) philosophers who hold that the fetus is nourished in the uterus by sucking on "a little piece of flesh."

6. *Empedocles debated the matter,* etc.: Reading *disputat ac rationes talis profert* with Giusta.

CHAPTER 7: *Growth in the Womb*

The Greeks and Romans did not share our view that there is a single common pattern to the child's growth in the womb, i.e., that normal human gestation takes nine months to complete, but that some children may be born "premature." Instead, with only a few exceptions, the ancients held to the idea that children are born an exact number of months after conception. The most common opinion—which lasted well into the Renaissance—was that children might be born seven or nine months after conception, but that "eighth-month" children were doomed. See Anne E. Hanson, "The Eight Month's Child and the Etiquette of Birth: *Obsit Omen!" Bulletin of the History of Medicine* 61 (1987) 589–602; Holt N. Parker, "Greek Embryological Calendars and a Fragment from the Lost Work of Damastes, *On the Care of Pregnant Women and of Infants," Classical Quarterly* 49 (1999): 515–34.

2. *seven:* There is much more about sevens in chapters 11 and 14 below. Varro produced a book called *Imagines* with 700 portraits of famous people (Pliny *Natural History* 35.11). It began with a discussion of the power of seven, which was likely one of Censorinus's sources. Some of it is quoted in Aulus Gellius *Attic Nights* 3.10. An entire book titled *On Sevens* was attributed to Hippocrates; see Jaap Mansfeld, *The Pseudo-Hippocratic Tract Peri hebdomadon Ch. 1–11 and Greek Philosophy* (Assen: Van Gorcum, 1971). Philo of Alexandria (*De opificio mundi* 89–128) gives a long discussion of the significance of the number seven, which shares many sources with Censorinus. There is an excellent annotated translation by David T. Runia, *Philo of Alexandria: On the Creation of the Cosmos according to Moses* (Leiden: Brill, 2001), esp. 264–65 on sources. Much of the material about sevens is also found in a long chapter in Macrobius *Commentary on the Dream of Scipio* 1.6. See also Pseudo-Iamblichus,

The Theology of Arithmetic, trans. Robin Waterfield (Grand Rapids: Phanes Press, 1988), 87–100.

5. *a woman can give birth in the seventh month:* The standard opinion. Theano: this citation only here. Aristotle *History of Animals* 583b33, 584a36, 584b2; *Generation of Animals* 772b6–9, 777a32. Diocles and Strato: Macrobius *Commentary on the Dream of Scipio* 1.6.65–66; Pseudo-Plutarch (Aëtius) *Opinions of the Philosophers* (*Placita*) 5.18 (*Moralia* 907f); Pseudo-Iamblichus *The Theology of Arithmetic* 48. Evenor: otherwise unknown. Empedocles: Pseudo-Plutarch (Aëtius) *Opinions of the Philosophers* (*Placita*) 5.18 (*Moralia* 907f); Proclus *Commentary on the Republic* 34.25–35.10 (Kroll). Epigenes: only here. Euryphon: only here.

8. *Epicharmus:* This citation only here. Diocles: see above. Aristole *Generation of Animals* 772b7–11 (cf. 775a1–4, 776a22); *History of Animals* 584a36–84b1, 583b31–35, 584b2–14. Epigenes: see above. Hippocrates *Eighth-Month Child* 2.1, 10.1 (7.438.3–11, 7.452.13 Littré = 165.6–16, 174.10 Joly = 82.21, 90.11–19 Grensemann); contradicted elsewhere (7.444.22–446.5 Littré; 96.5–11 Grenseman; 169.16–170.3 Joly).

CHAPTER 8: *The Origins of Astrology*

For an introduction, see Tamsyn Barton, *Ancient Astrology* (New York: Routledge, 1994). Much of Latin astrological and astronomical lore can be found in *Manilius: Astronomica,* trans. G. P. Goold (Cambridge, Mass.: Harvard University Press, 1977).

3. *"aspects":* A very clear explanation of the basic principals that are still used in astrology.

4. *Zodiac:* Cf. Cicero *On Divination* 2.89.

wandering stars: The planets.

6. *when the Sun is in the third sign, that is, with one sign in between:* The Greeks and Romans counted inclusively. So, for example, the phrase from the New Testament "on the third day" indicates Friday–Saturday–Sunday.

CHAPTER 9: *The Teachings of the Pythagoreans*

For an introduction, see Charles H. Kahn, *Pythagoras and the Pythagoreans: A Brief History* (Indianapolis: Hackett, 2001). For a detailed treatment, see Walter Burkert, *Lore and Science in Ancient Pythagoreanism* (Cambridge, Mass.: Harvard University Press, 1972). For the theories of gestation referred to here, see the works cited under chapters 6 and 7.

1. *Tubero: Tubero, or On Human Generation,* a lost work, named after the main interlocutor, L. Aelius Tubero, friend of Cicero. Nearly all that we know about it comes from Censorinus. The fragments are collected in *I logistorici Varroniani,* ed. Ettore Bolisani (Padova: Tipo. del Messaggero, 1937).

CHAPTER 10: *Harmony and Music*

Ancient music theory was a highly developed branch of mathematics. A superb and approachable introduction is M. L. West, *Ancient Greek Music* (Oxford: Oxford University Press, 1992). The sources have been gathered in exemplary English translations: *Greek Musical Writings,* 2 vols., ed. Andrew Barker (Cambridge: Cambridge University Press, 1984). See the excellent translation by Jon Solomon, *Ptolemy: Harmonics* (Leiden: Brill, 2000). Nearly all the terms that Censorinus used (here in quotations marks) are Greek.

7. *Plato:* These terms are not in fact used by Plato. Censorinus has in mind the immensely complicated series of ratios set out in Plato's *Timaeus* esp. 36b1–6. The *dialeimma* (Pseudo-Aristotle *Problems* 921b10), usually just *leimma,* is a microtone (in the ratio of 253:243), also called the *diesis.* For these terms, see *Greek Musical Writings,* ed. Andrew Barker, 38n36, 44n65, 58–60nn17–18, 203n54, 217, 222–24, 227–28, 296–98, 313–14, 337, 496, 528n205; Macrobius *Commentary on the Dream of Scipio* 2.1.21–23; also Proclus *In Timaeum* 2.179.11–180.15 (Diehl), etc.

8. *For he stretched strings of equal thickness:* This famous experiment does not work in the way Censorinus explained it. It is not strings stretched with differing *weights,* but rather differing *lengths* of strings which produce the

stated intervals. Censorinus correctly reports the way that differing *lengths* of pipes produce a musical fifth, fourth, and octave. This might make an attractive grade-school experiment. For similar accounts of Pythagoras's discoveries, see *Greek Musical Writings* 256–58 (Nicomachus), 495 (Aristeides Quintilianus); Macrobius *Commentary on The Dream of Scipio* 2.1.8–14; Iamblichus *Life of Pythagoras* 115–21.

epitrite: literally "plus a third," i.e., $4/3 = 1 \, 1/3$.

9. *hemiolon:* "half and whole," i.e., $1 \, 1/2$. For these terms, see Plato *Timaeus* 36a6; Pseudo-Aristotle *Problems* 919b1; *Greek Musical Writings* (Aristides Quintilianus) 499; Macrobius *Commentary on The Dream of Scipio* 2.1.15–20.

10. *flute:* The ancient "flute" (Greek *aulos,* Latin *tibia*) was a reed instrument with two pipes.

CHAPTER 11: *Harmony in the Womb*

See the works cited for chapters 6 and 7 above.

3. *Pythagoras:* See Diogenes Laertius 8.29; Proclus *Commentary on Plato's Republic* 13.34 (attributed to Empedocles).

5. *perfect numbers:* See Plato *Republic* 546b4; Euclid *Elements* Book 7, definition 23; Macrobius *Commentary on the Dream of Scipio* 1.6.16–17, etc.; Thomas L. Heath, *A History of Greek Mathematics* (Oxford: Oxford University Press, 1921), I, 74–75.

6. *Solon:* Solon 27 in *Greek Elegiac Poetry: From the Seventh to the Fifth Centuries,* ed. Douglas E. Gerber (Cambridge, Mass.: Harvard University Press, 1999), 148–51.

Etruscans: On the lost books of the Etruscans, see chapters 4.13, 14.6, and 17.5–6; also Cicero *Divination* 1.72: Livy 5.14.4, 5.11.5; Macrobius *Saturnalia* 3.7.2, 3.20.3; Festus 358, 359 (Lindsay); Servius on *Aeneid* 8.398.

Hippocrates: See esp. *Fleshes* 19 in *Hippocrates, Vol. VIII,* trans. David Potter (Cambridge, Mass.: Harvard University Press, 1995), 158–65.

7. *based on seven:* Whereas the ratios based on six work nicely ($6 + 8 + 9 + 12$), the harmonies based on seven do not, and Censorinus is forced to do some fudging. He does not specify the intervening stages, but keeping,

as he said, to the same harmonies, we would have $7 + 9\frac{1}{3}$ (3:4, a musical fourth) + $10\frac{1}{2}$ (2:3, a musical fifth) + 14 (1:2, an octave), giving a total of $40\frac{5}{6}$, which Censorinus rounds down to an even forty and multiplied by seven to get the total of two hundred and eighty days, which equals forty weeks. He then says that it is really not forty full weeks, but thirty-nine weeks plus a day: $39 \times 7 = 273$ (+ 1 = 274), so that the result matches up with $\frac{3}{4}$ of a year of 365 days (273 $\frac{3}{4}$ days).

fortieth days: Censorinus seems to be our only source for these laws and festivals. However, for similar prohibitions, see R. Parker, *Miasma* (Oxford: Oxford University Press, 1983), esp. 48–49; Susan Guettel Cole, *Landscapes, Gender, and Ritual Space* (Berkeley: University of California Press, 2004), 104–8.

forty days after birth: Aristotle *History of Animals* 587b2–5.

9. *and some odd hours:* See chapters 19.2 and 20.10, and note 22.4 below.

10. *the experience of the doctors:* See esp. Hippocrates *Fleshes* 19 (cited above); *Nature of the Child* 13 (in *Hippocratic Writings,* 325–26). For a full list, see Parker, "Greek Embryological Calendars," 521n17.

efflux and miscarriage: For the distinction, see Parker, "Greek Embryological Calendars," 521n28.

11. *even numbers:* For the Pythagorean Table of Opposites, where "odd" is associated with "male" and "right," etc., and "even" with "female" and "left," etc., see Aristotle *Metaphysics* A5, 986a21–26; Kirk-Raven-Schofield, *The Presocratic Philosophers,* 336–39.

CHAPTER 12: *Harmony in the Mind and Body*

1. *Socrates:* Actually, Plato says just the opposite (e.g., *Laws* 653d–654a, 664e–665a), but cf. *Philebus* 17b on sound; and *Symposium* 215c for the power of music.

Aristoxenus: Cf. Quintilian 1.20.22 citing Aristoxenus for rhythm (marked by beating time) and melody (movement of the voice); for Aristoxenus's surviving works, see *Greek Musical Writings,* II, 119–89; also quoted by Lactantius (probably drawing on the same sources as Censorinus) *On* the *Workmanship of God* (*de opificio Dei*) 16 for the notion of harmony in the soul and body.

Theophrastus: Greek Musical Writings, II, 111–12.

2. *to please the gods:* See, e.g., Plato *Laws* 653c. For the place of music in Roman life, see John G. Landels, *Music in Ancient Greece and Rome* (London: Routledge, 1999).

plays: For the Romans' story of the origins of their theatrical games, see Livy 7.2; Valerius Maximus 2.4.4; Augustine *City of God* 4.1, 26, 31, citing Varro, whose lost *De scaenicis originibus* is the source for all of these. See also notes 17.7–8 below.

flute: For use in prayers, see Horace *Odes* 1.36. For triumphs, see Plutarch *Marcellus* 22.4 (ovation); Cassius Dio 7.21.11; Florus 1.18.10.

lyre: For the story of the invention of the lyre, see *Homeric Hymn to Hermes.*

the "Little Festival" of Minerva: On 13 June, was sacred to flute players, who were essential to a proper Roman sacrifice. See Livy 9.30.5–10 for the origin of the festival; also Valerius Maximus 2.5.4; Plutarch *Roman Questions* 55 (Mor. 277e–278b); Festus 134.4 (Lindsay). For a pleasant retelling of the story, see Ovid *Fasti* 6.652–710. For the Ides, see the glossary above.

3. *though Epicurus disagreed:* See Epicurus in Diogenes Laertius 10.124, 139; an English translation in *The Essential Epicurus,* trans. Eugene O'Connor (Buffalo: Prometheus Books, 1993), 63, 69. The main exposition of Epicurus is Lucretius 3.396–783.

steersman: The Greeks and Romans set the tempo for both rowing and marching to flutes and trumpets; see Thucydides 5.7; Aulus Gellius 1.11.1–9, 17–19; Quintilian 1.10.14–16. See also Xenophon *Constitution of the Spartans* 13.7–8; Polybius 4.20.6; Cicero *Tusculan Disputations* 2.37. The Chigi vase shows Spartan troops on the march to the music of an aulos player.

4. *Pythagoras:* Iamblichus *Life of Pythagoras* 114; Seneca *On Anger* 3.9.2; Cicero *Tusculan Disputations* 4.3; Quintilian 9.4.12; Plutarch *On Isis and Osiris* (Mor. 384a).

Asclepiades: See Martianus Capella *The Wedding of Philology and Mercury* 9.926 (356 Willis).

Herophilus: Heinrich Von Staden, *Herophilus: The Art of Medicine in Early Alexandria* (Cambridge: Cambridge University Press, 1988), 360–61, 393.

CHAPTER 13: *Harmony in the Universe*

1. *sing in chorus the sweetest melody possible, but inaudible to us:* This is the famous Music of the Spheres. For Pythagoras's cosmos, see Plato *Republic* 10.617b; Aristotle *On the Heavens* 290b12–291a28 (who calls the idea beautiful but impossible); Cicero *On the Nature of the Gods* 3.27 (cf. 2.19); *Republic* 6.18–19; Pliny *Natural History* 2.83–84; Macrobius *Commentary on the Dream of Scipio* 2.1.1–8; Quintilian 1.10.12. For summaries, see D. R. Dicks, *Early Greek Astronomy to Aristotle* (London: Thames & Hudson, 1970), 62–76.

2. *Eratosthenes:* 252,000 stadia [about 29,060 miles]. Eratosthenes' measurement of the circumference of the earth is one of the greatest intellectual feats of antiquity. The report is that he had been told that when the sun was directly overhead on the summer solstice in Aswan, Egypt, it shone directly down a well, casting no shadow. On the same day at Alexandria, 500 Greek stadia to the north, he set up a pole and measured the angle of the shadow thrown by the sun.

When he found out that the angle was nearly $1/50$ of a complete circle (7.2°), he multiplied the 500 stades by 50 to get the full circumference of the earth: 500 stades × 50 = 25000 stades = 29,060 miles. Eratosthenes' calculation was remarkably close: the standard figure for the diameter of the Earth at the equator is 24,900 miles. See Dicks, *Early Greek Astronomy to Aristotle*, 62–76. For text of Cleomedes, who gives the fullest account, see *Cleomedes' Lectures on Astronomy: A Translation of The Heavens,* ed. Alan C. Bowen and Robert B. Todd (Berkeley: University of California Press, 2004), and literature cited there. See also Jacques Dutka, "Eratosthenes' Measurement of the Earth Reconsidered," *Archive for History of Exact Sciences* 46 (1993) 55–66.

the Olympic stadium: It is this measurement that gave the name to the most important race at Olympia, thence to the area for watching that race, and thence to our word "stadium." The Olympic stadium (stadion) was 600

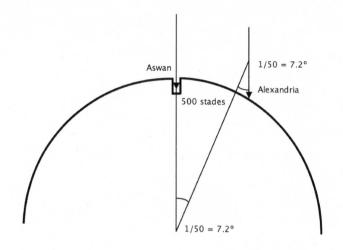

Aswan

1/50 = 7.2°

Alexandria

500 stades

1/50 = 7.2°

Olympic feet, and the foot involved was said to be that of Hercules, who had extra big feet—about 12.6 inches (320 mm). The stadium (or stade) was therefore about 630 English feet (192 m).

3. *Earth to the Moon was about 126,000 stadia:* About 14,530 miles. Pythagoras's calculations were much too small. At its closest point (perigee) the moon is about 225,700 miles away, at its furthest (apogee), about 252,000 miles.

Stilbon, etc.: For these poetic names of the planets, see Pseudo-Aristotle *On the Cosmos* 392a23–31; Cicero *Nature of the Gods* 2.52–53; Geminus 1.24–30 (Heath, *Greek Astronomy,* 129–30); Pseudo-Plutarch (Aëtius) *Opinions of the Philosophers (Placita)* 2.15 (*Moralia* 889b); Hyginus *Astronomy* 2.42, 4.15–19. Stilbon means "Gleamer"; Phosphoros, "Light-Bringer" (hence the name of the element); Pyrois, "Fiery"; Phaethon, "Radiant" (also the name of the son of Helios); Phaenon, "Shiner."

5. *Dorylaus:* Found only here.

seven-stringed lyre: Cf. Philo of Alexandria *De opificio mundi* 126 = *On the Creation of the Cosmos according to Moses* 79.

CHAPTER 14: *Crisis Years and the Length of Life*

1. *climacteric:* Relating to steps on a ladder. For the theory of climacteric years, which Varro attributed to the Chaldeans, see Aulus Gellius 3.10.9; Pliny *Natural History* 7.161. For a later text, see Firmicus Maternus 4.20.3 in *Ancient Astrology: Theory and Practice: Matheseos libri VIII,* trans. Jean Rhys Bram (Park Ridge, N.J.: Noyes Press, 1975).

2. *Varro:* See Servius on *Aeneid* 5.295.

boys (pueri): Folk etymology, as is that for *iuvenes* (youths), but *sen-*ior, *sen-esco,* and *sen-ium* obviously share a root.

3. *Hippocrates . . . seven stages:* Aristotle also makes use of this scheme, *History of Animals* 544b26, 570a30, 581a14, 582a17; *Politics* 1335b22. For sevens, see notes above on chapters 7 and 11.

Shakespeare inherited this scheme of "The Seven Ages of Man":

> *All the world's a stage,*
> *And all the men and women merely players;*
> *They have their exits and their entrances,*
> *And one man in his time plays many parts,*
> *His acts being seven ages.*

JACQUES, *As You Like It,* II.vii.139f.

4. *Solon:* Solon 23; note 11.6 above.

5. *Staseas:* See below. Eighty-four years may have been proverbial; see Plautus *The Merchant* 673.

Olympic runners and charioteers: That is, sheer momentum carries them onward, even after the end of the race.

7. *goat-ize:* A connection is being made between Greek *trag-izein,* "bleat like a goat/have the voice break," and "smell like a goat." See Aristotle *History of Animals* 581a17; *Generation of Animals* 788a1; Pseudo-Aristotle *Problems* 789a22–25.

8. *"pre-ephebe,"* etc.: These words, known primarily from the grammar-

ians, were not in general use, and are not technical or precise terms, as Censorinus implies.

11. *forty-ninth:* Cf. Macrobius *Commentary on the Dream of Scipio* 1.6.75.

12. *Plato . . . eighty-one years:* Not in Plato, but there was a tradition that Plato lived to be eighty-one: Cicero *On Old Age* 13; Seneca *Letters* 58.31. See below, note 15.1.

13. *Apollo:* For seven equaling Apollo and nine equaling the Muses, cf. Plutarch *Symposium Questions* 9.3 (*Moralia* 738d), which concludes with some healthy laughter at all such stuff.

pathos: Iamblichus *Pythagorian Life* 114; cf. Aulus Gellius 1.26.11, 4.13; and chapter 12.4 for madness and music.

14. *sixty-three:* For the dangers of sixty-three, see Aulus Gellius 15.7.

16. *Aristotle:* See Diogenes Laertius 5.6 and Aulus Gellius 13.5.1.

CHAPTER 15: *The Praise of Caerellius*

1. *Caerellius:* Since Caerellius has passed 49 but is not yet 56 (the next climacteric year), he was born between 182 and 189 AD. See *Prosopographia imperii romani saec. I. II. III.* (Berlin and Leipzig: Walter de Gruyter, 1933–), under Caerellius 156.

Plato: See chapter 14.12.

2. *Dionysius of Heraclea:* Diogenes Laertius 7.166–67.

Diogenes the Cynic: Diogenes Laertius 6.76; cf. Lucian *Dialogues of the Dead* 4.2 (Lucian 77.4[21].2 Macleod).

Eratosthenes: 82, according to Pseudo-Lucian *Octagenarians* (*Makrobioi*) 27; 80, according to the Byzantine encyclopedia, *Suda* (403 Adler).

Xenocrates: 84, according to Pseudo-Lucian *Octagenarians* 20; 82, according to Diogenes Laertius 4.14.

3. There seem to have been a number of collections of "Long-Lived People" of which the Pseudo-Lucian *Octagenarians* (*Makrobioi*) is the best known.

Carneades: Valerius Maximus 8.7.ext.5; only 85, according to Pseudo-Lucian *Octagenarians* (*Makrobioi*) 20 and Diogenes Laertius 4.65.

Cleanthes: Pseudo-Lucian *Octagenarians* (*Makrobioí*) 19 and Diogenes Laertius 7.176.

Xenophanes: At least to 92, as he says in a poem, Elegy 8 (= Diogenes Laertius 9.18–19); 91, according to Pseudo-Lucian *Octagenarians* (*Makrobioí*) 20.

Democritus: 104, according to Pseudo-Lucian *Octagenarians* (*Makrobioí*) 18; 109, according to Diogenes Laertius 9.43 (cf. 9.39).

Isocrates: 99, according to Pseudo-Lucian *Octagenarians* (*Makrobioí*) 23; Plutarch *Lives of the Ten Orators* (*Moralia* 837f); Pausanias 1.18.8; 98 or 99, according to Cicero *On Old Age* 13.

Gorgias: 107, according to Cicero *On Old Age* 13. 108, according to Pseudo-Lucian *Octagenarians* (*Makrobioí*) 23; Valerius Maximus 8.13.ext.3; Pliny *Natural History* 7.156; Quintilian 3.1.8; 109, according to Athenaeus 12.209.21–24.

6. *Very Important Audiences: Auditoria sacra:* Censorinus implies that Caerellius has spoken before the Emperor himself. Cf. Ausonius *Gratiarum actio* (*opuscula* 24) 45; Symmachus 2.30.1, 8.17.

CHAPTER 16: *Time and Eternity*

The second half of the book now turns from "birth" to "day," and to time in general.

3. *Eon: Aeon,* Greek *aion,* is connected with the word *aei* ("always"). For the eon, see Aristotle *On the Heavens* 279a22–30; Varro *Latin Language* 6.11; cf. Plato *Timaeus* 37e–38d. See Eli Maor, *To Infinity and Beyond: A Cultural History of the Infinite* (Princeton: Princeton University Press, 1991); Wilbur R. Knorr, "Infinity and Continuity: The Interaction of Mathematics and Philosophy in Antiquity," in *Infinity and Continuity in Ancient and Medieval Thought*, ed. Norman Kretzmann, 112–45 (Ithaca: Cornell University Press, 1982).

4. *past, present, future:* For Aristotle on time, see esp. *Physics* 251b11–29. For the language, cf. Seneca *On the Brevity of Life* 10.2; Plutarch *On the E at Delphi* 19 (*Moralia* 392e–f).

6. *one short hour in winter:* See chapter 23.6. Since the Romans divided the period of sunrise to sunset into twelve hours, hours in winter were shorter. For the expression, see Plautus *Pseudolus* 1304.

CHAPTER 17: *Ages and Centuries. The Roman Secular Games*

16.7: *Ages of Gold and Silver:* Hesiod *Works and Days* 109–73.

17.2. *"age":* Lat. *saeculum,* whose basic meaning is "a generation (of people); an age."

Heraclitus: See Plutarch *On the Failure of Oracles* 11 (*Moralia* 415e) and Philo Judaeus frag. *Questiones in Genesim* 6.14 (p. 20 §5 Harris).

from one human "sowing" to the next "sowing": As Plutarch (above) explains, "time in which a begetter shows a begetter begotten from him," that is, from a man's birth to the when he becomes (or could become) a grandfather (15 + 15 years).

Herodicus: This might be either Herodicus of Babylon (also called of Seleucia), a grammarian and pupil of Crates, probably second century BC; or Herodicus of Selymbria, a doctor of the fifth century BC.

3. *Herodotus:* Actually, 120 years, according to Herodotus 1.163; Cicero *On Old Age* 69; and Valerius Maximus 8.13.ext.4. And 150 years, according to Pliny *Natural History* 7.154 and Pseudo-Lucian *Octagenarians* (*Makrobioi*) 10. And 300 years according to Silius Italicus 3.398.

Ephorus: Pliny *Natural History* 7.155; Servius on *Aeneid* 8.51.

4. *Epigenes* and *Berosos:* Pliny *Natural History* 7.160.

5. *Etruscans:* See above, chapters 4.13, 11.6, and 14.6. Censorinus is our only source for this Etruscan reckoning.

6. *Varro:* Probably in the lost *De Saeculis,* part of *Antiquitates rerum humanarum et divinarum.*

Ninth and Tenth cycles: According to Plutarch *Sulla* 7.3–5, the Etruscans had only eight cycles, and a new one began in 88 BC (cf. Diodorus Siculus 38/39.5). According to Servius on *Eclogues* 9.46, the prophet Vulcanius declared that the comet at Caesar's funeral Games of 44 BC signified the end of the ninth cycle and the beginning of the tenth; but since this was a divine secret, he died immediately. The story was supposedly in Book II of Augustus's autobiography.

7. *Secular Games:* Theatrical games and sacrifices apparently originally held to avert plague, but later associated with the end of a *saeculum,* variously understood. They were also called the Tarentine Games from an association with a deep sacrificial pit in the Campus Martius in Rome, called the Tarentum. Censorinus's account is somewhat confused, but the history of the Secular Games was subject to rewriting to fit in with new traditions. Games in 509 and 346 BC were legendary. The next in 249 BC were probably the first historical games, followed by those in 146 BC. The Civil War interfered with any regular cyclical celebration, and in 17 BC, Augustus consulted the Sybilline books, which happily gave precedents for the timing of his celebration and fixed a *saeculum* at 110 years. Claudius tried a new calendar in AD 47 to mark the 800th birthday of Rome. Domitian reset the clock with games in 88 (six years early), then Septimius Severus gave them for the last time in 204 (by the time of the next scheduled games, 314, Constantine had converted to Christianity). See Livy *Periocha* 49; Valerius Maximus 4.5.5; Horace *Carmen Saeculare*; Festus 400–401 (Lindsay). The long inscriptions from Augustus's and Septimius Serverus's games are translated in *Roman Civilization. Sourcebook II: The Empire,* eds. Naphtali Lewis and Meyer Reinhold (New York: Harper & Row, 1966), 56–61, 558–60 (note, however, this translation does not include certain new material and restorations). The new edition by Bärbel Schnegg-Köhler, *Die augusteischen Säkularspiele* (Archiv für Religionsgeschichte Vol. 4; München and Leipzig: Saur, 2002) supersedes all others. The other sources are gathered in Giovanni Battista Pighi, *De Ludis Saecularibus Populi Romani Quiritium Libri Sex*, 2nd ed. (Amsterdam: P. Schippers, 1965), which is in need of an update.

Censorinus lists three items of information: the authority, the date in years after the foundation of Rome (AUC: *ab urbe condita*), and the two consuls for that year. The text here has suffered some losses due to the nature of the material, and I have followed the emendations of Klaus Sallmann, *Censorini De die natali liber ad Q. Caerellium* (Leipzig: Teubner, 1983), which give the general sense. His additions to the text are printed in angled brackets, thus ‹ . . . ›. However, his text incorrectly prints CCXCVIIII (299 AUC = 457 BC). He renders that date as 456 BC (*Cenorinus: Betrachtungen zum Tag der Geburt* [Weinheim: VCH, 1988], 125), in which he is followed by Rapisarda (1991, 206), who, however, gives 298 AUC in his translation (90). The date must be 298 AUC = 456 BC for the listed consuls. The text was corrected by the editors Jahn (1845) and Hultsch (1867); right in Pighi (1965, 38).

Censorinus's dates come from several different sources. The records of the Council of Fifteen give 456 BC, 344 BC, 236 BC, 126 BC; these dates seem to have been in part rewritten to match up with 110 year intervals back from Augustus's games. The date of 344 BC seems to be a mistake; one expects 346 BC, and Lachmann emended the text accordingly. The annalists give 509 BC, 346 BC, 249 BC, 149 BC or 146 BC. Censorinus cites Antias, Gnaeus Gellius, Hermina, and Varro. Since the matter is so complex, I have arranged the results in a table.

Authority
Year of Rome [year BC]
Consuls

1.	‹Antias›	Board of 15
	245 [509]	298 [456]
	Valerius Publicola	M. Valerius
	‹Sp. Lucretius›	Spurius Verginius
‹2.›	‹Antias›	Board of 15
	408 [346]	410 [344]
	M. Valerius Corvus	‹C. Marcius Rutilius›
	C. Poetilius	‹T. Manlius Imperisosus›
3.	Antias and Livy	‹Board of 15›
	‹505› [249]	518 [236]
	P. Claudius Pulcher	P. Cornelius Lentulus
	L. Iunius Pullus	C. Licinius Varus

4. a.	Antias, Varro, Livy	Board of 15
	605 [149]	628 [126]
	L. Marcius Censorinus	M. Aemilius Lepidus
	Manius Manilius	L. Aurelius Orestes
b.	Piso, Gellius, Hemina	
	608 [146]	
	Gn. Cornelius Lentulus	
	L. Mummius Achaicus	

8. *Antias:* A major source for Livy and other historians, but nothing is directly preserved.

Varro . . . The Early Theater at Rome: See Servius on *Georgics* 1.19. These are the games of 249 BC.

Council of Fifteen: One of the Roman colleges of priests, in charge of the Sibylline Books and performing ritual acts for the state.

9. *Horace in the song which was sung at the Secular Games:* Horace's *Carmen Saeculare*.

11. *L. Marcius Censorinus:* Possibly an ancestor.

13. *Piso:* Lucius Calpurnius Piso Frugi. His *Annales* are lost. His chronology is four years off; these are the consuls for 158 BC while the year 600 AUC was actually 154 BC.

14. *mummies:* For what the Greeks and Romans thought they knew about mummification, see Herodotus 2.85–90 and Diodorus Siculus 1.91.

heart: For this belief, see Pliny *Natural History* 11.184. The unit of weight is the drachma, about one-tenth of an ounce.

15. *twelve vultures:* See Livy 1.7.1.

1,200 years: This works out to AD 447. As Rome was sacked by Alaric the Goth in AD 410, and the traditional end of ancient Rome came in 476 with the deposition of the last emperor, Romulus Augustulus, Vettius's prophesy seems fairly accurate. In the fifth century, people seem to have become uncomfortably aware of the prophecy. It is mentioned by Claudian *Gothic War* 266 (written 402 AD), and Sidonius Apollinaris *Carmen* 7.55

(written 456). So remarked Gibbon, chap. 35, in *Decline and Fall of the Roman Empire* (New York: Modern Library, 1932), II: 298:

> As early as the time of Cicero and Varro it was the opinion of the Roman augurs that the *twelve vultures* which Romulus had seen, represented the *twelve centuries* assigned for the fatal period of his city. This prophecy, disregarded perhaps in the season of health and prosperity, inspired the people with gloomy apprehensions when the twelfth century, clouded with disgrace and misfortune, was almost elapsed; and even posterity must acknowledge with some surprise that the arbitrary interpretation of an accidental or fabulous circumstance has been seriously verified in the downfall of the Western empire.

CHAPTER 18: *The Great Year*

1. *Great Year:* A Great Year is one in which various sets of heavenly bodies all return simultaneously to an original position. The rotation of the earth, the rotation of the moon about the earth, and the rotation of the earth around the sun have different periods, and astronomers have often tried to find some common multiple of all three. Since a standard lunar month is slightly over 29 1/2 days (29.5306 days = 29 days, 12 hours, 44 minutes, 3 seconds), and a year is slightly less than 365 1/4 days (365.2422 days = 365 days, 5 hours, 48 minutes, 45 seconds), there will be discrepancies in any system. In fact, even calculating a year at exactly 365 $\frac{1}{4}$ days and a lunar month at exactly 29 $\frac{1}{2}$ days still means that the lowest common multiple for a Great Year would be 236 years (= 2922 lunar months = 86,199 days).

The Greek astronomer Geminus (c. AD 50) dealt with the Great Year in his *Introduction to Astronomy,* chap. 8. Portions of Geminus are translated by Thomas L. Heath, *Greek Astronomy* (London: Dent, 1932; repr. New York: Dover, 1991), 140–41, and the mind-boggling business is made as clear as it can by Heath's *Aristarchus of Samos: The Ancient Copernicus* (Oxford: Oxford University Press, 1913; repr. New York: Dover, 1981), 284–97. See also

Pseudo-Plutarch (Aëtius) *Opinions of the Philosophers* (*Placita*) 2.32 (*Moralia* 892c). For Roman discussions of various ideas about the Great Year, see Cicero *On the Nature of the Gods* 2.51; *On the Ends of Good and Evil* 2.102; Macrobius *Saturnalia* 1.14.4; *Commentary on the Dream of Scipio* 2.11.5–10.

2. *triennium:* Two years counted inclusively.

Liber: The Roman name for Dionysus/Bacchus. For *trieteris,* see Statius *Thebaid* 4.723, 7.93, etc. Cf. Virgil *Aeneid* 4.302; Ovid *Metamorphoses* 6.587, etc.

5. *2,922 complete days:* So 365 $\frac{1}{4}$ days × 8 = 2922. The lunar months are close, but not exact, since 29 $\frac{1}{2}$ days (per lunar month) × 99 = 2920 $\frac{1}{2}$ (just 1 $\frac{1}{2}$ days short). See Geminus 8.27–35 for this type of Great Year. Despite what Censorinus says, an eight-year cycle was not in general use in Greece.

Dositheus: Mentioned by Pliny *Natural History* 18.312. The rest are otherwise unknown.

6. *Pythian Games:* Second after the Olympics in importance. Originally they consisted of a hymn sung at Delphi in honor of Apollo, every eight years. The games were refounded officially in 582 BC with other musical and athletic contests. For the original eight-year period, see Plutarch *Greek Questions* 12 (*Moralia* 293c); *Obsolescence of Oracles* 21 (*Moralia* 421c); Pausanias 10.7.

8. *Meton:* He introduced his cycle in 432 BC to reconcile the Athenian lunar and solar civic calendars; see below and Aristophanes *Birds* 992–1019 (a mocking portrait); Diodorus Siculus 12.36.2–4; Aratus 752–57; Geminus 8.48–58 (Heath, *Aristarchus of Samos,* 293–95; *Greek Astronomy,* 140–41). G. J. Toomer, "Meton," in *Dictionary of Scientific Biography,* ed. Charles Coulston Gillispie (New York: Scribner, 1974), 9:337–40. In Meton's system, there are 19 years, 235 months (125 with 30 days, 110 with 29 days), and 6940 days. Accordingly, each year works out at 365 $\frac{5}{19}$ days (see note 19.2). Using modern figures, 19 years equal 6939 days, 14 hours, 26 minutes; while 235 lunar months equal 6939 days, 16 hours, 35 minutes—only a little over two hours' difference.

Philolaus: His Great Year contains approximately 2 revolutions of Saturn (29.46 years), 5 of Jupiter (11.86 years), 31 of Mars (1.88 years), and 729 of the Moon. A 59-year cycle is also attributed to Oinopides of Chios by Pseudo-Plutarch (Aëtius) *Opinions of the Philosophers* (*Placita*) 2.32 (*Moralia* 892c).

Callippus: Geminus 8.59 (his followers); also mentioned by Pliny *Natural History* 18.312; Vitruvius 9.6.3. Callippus multiplies Meton's Great Year by four, to remove the extra quarter of a day ($19 \times 365 \frac{1}{4} = 6939 \frac{3}{4}$; $6939 \frac{3}{4} \times 4 = 27759$); cf. note 19.2 below. See Heath, *Aristarchus of Samos,* 295–96; *Greek Astronomy,* 140–41.

Democritus: For his book called *The Great Year; or, the Astronomical Calendar,* see Diogenes Laertius 9.48; also Vitruvius 9.6.3.

9. *Hipparchus:* Hipparchus doubles Callippus's Great Year (which was already four times Meton's Great Year). See Heath, *Aristarchus of Samos,* 296–97; G. J. Toomer, "Hipparchus," in *Dictionary of Scientific Biography* 15 (Supplement 1), ed. Charles Coulston Gillispie (New York: Scribner, 1978), 207–24. Hipparchus was praised by Pliny *Natural History* 2.53, 2.57, 2.95, 2.188, 2.247; mentioned by Servius on *Aeneid* 5.49; Columella 9.14.12.

10. *Thoth:* The first month of the Egyptian calendar, named for the God of Speech, who invented the calendar. On the rising of Sirius, see note 21.10.

1,461 years: I.e., $365 \frac{1}{4} \times 4$.

heliacal: E.g., Geminus 8.15; Pseudo-Plutarch (Aëtius) *Opinions of the Philosophers* (*Placita*) 2.32.3 (*Moralia* 892c).

Year of God: The phrase (in Greek) is otherwise unattested.

11. *Aristotle:* There is nothing exactly like this in the surviving works of Aristotle, but cf. *Meteorologica* 352a28. Of the other cited passages, Aristotle frags. 18 and 19 (Rose) = Philo *On the Eternity of the World* 10–12, 20–24 do not mention a Great Year; Cicero *On the Nature of the Gods* 2.20 describes a similar Great Year, but does not attribute it to Aristotle.

Cataclysm and *Ekpyrosis:* See Plato *Timaeus* 22c; Diogenes Laertius 7.141–42 on Zeno; Cicero *Republic* 6.23; Seneca *Natural Questions* 3.29; Macrobius *Commentary on the Dream of Scipio* 2.10.12–13; Firmius Maternus 3.1.9; Servius on *Eclogues* 4.10, citing the lost work of Nigidius Figulus *On the Gods,* Book 4; see also Augustine *City of God* 12.10.12 (on pagan beliefs).

Aristarchus, etc.: Censorinus is our only source for most of these calculations for the Great Great Years. Aristarchus is famed as the first to theorize a heliocentric solar system; see Heath, *Aristarchus of Samos,* 299–316.

Aristarchus thought this took 2434 solar years: Most manuscripts of Censorinus read 2484 here (II CCCCCLXXXXIIII; see Sallmann's ed. for details). However, as Tannery showed, the proper figure needs to be 2434 (II CCCCCXXXXIIII); an L has got in by mistake. The Babylonians had already observed that lunar eclipses seemed to occur every 223 lunar months, calculated as 6,585 ⅓ days; see Otto Neugebauer, *A History of Ancient Mathematical Astronomy* (Berlin & New York: Springer-Verlag, 1975), 1:497. Aristarchus was working with a period called the *exeligmos* ("countermarch, turn of the wheel"), which took this Chaldean figure and multiplied it by three to eliminate the fraction, and so got a period of 669 lunar months or 19,756 days, that is, 54 4/45 years; see Geminus 18.1–3; Ptolemy, *Almagest* 1.1.270 Heiberg, trans. G. J. Toomer, *Ptolemy's Almagest* (Princeton: Princeton University Press, 1998), 175. To eliminate *this* fraction, Aristarchus multiplied 54 4/45 by 45 to get a Great Great Year of 2,434 years. For the complete calculations, see Paul Tannery, "La grande année d' Aristarche de Samos," *Mémoires scientifiques* (Toulouse: E. Privat, 1912), 2:79–96; Rapisarda, *Censorini De die natali liber,* 229–300; explained by Heath, *Aristarchus of Samos,* 314–15. See also note 19.2.

For Aretes, see chapter 21.3. Pseudo-Plutarch (Aëtius) *Opinions of the Philosophers (Placita)* 2.32 *(Moralia* 892c) gives Heraclitus's Great Year as 18,000. The figure 10,800 probably is based on 30 x 360; that is, each "day" of Great Year (360 = days in a rounded solar year = number of degrees in a circle) lasts one human generation (30 years). The number is probably Babylonian in origin. Censorinus throws in the mythological Linus and Orpheus for good measure. Cassandrus is mentioned by Cicero *On Divination* 2.88.

12. *Olympiads:* The first traditionally dates to 776 BC. Here Censorinus gives the exact date of his book for the first time.

13. *lustrum:* The entire Roman people were purified with an ancient sacrifice of a pig, a sheep, and a cow. Livy 1.44, citing Fabius Pictor, gives the

details of Servius's first lustration in 566 BC. Livy 3.22, 10.47, 24.43 gives the later history of the lustrum. See also Dionysius of Halicarnassus 4.22; Varro *On Agriculture* 2.1.10; Valerius Maximus 3.4.3; Florus *Epitome of Roman History* 1.6.3.

15. *Capitoline Games*: Suetonius *Domitian* 4.8–9. Greek-style games with athletic and musical competitions, dedicated to Jupiter of the Capitoline Hill in Rome, and held every four years.

thirty-ninth Capitoline Games: Again, AD 238.

CHAPTER 19: *The Year*

2. *Callippus 365 [1/4] days*: Reading *et ‹partem diei quartam›* with Rapisarda's edition. Censorinus is listing the approximations in order of increasing length, and something has clearly fallen out: the *et* is dangling and does not link the names elsewhere in this list. Sallmann does not have the addition in his text or translation, but acknowledges that it is likely in his notes: *Cenorinus: Betrachtungen zum Tag der Geburt,* 131n4. Geminus (8.4) and the figures for Callippus's Great Year (note 18.8 above) make it clear that Callippus operated with a year of exactly 365 $\frac{1}{4}$ days. See Heath, *Aristarchus of Samos,* 295–96.

Aristarchus of Samos, the same number plus $\frac{1}{1623}$ of a day [365 $\frac{1}{4}$ + $\frac{1}{1623}$ days]: Aristarchus calculated that for the great period of the *exeligmos* (see above on note 18.11) of 669 lunar months = 19,756 days = 54 $\frac{4}{45}$ years, the year must equal 19,756 divided by 54 $\frac{4}{5}$ days = 365 $\frac{305}{1217}$ days. This in turn could be expressed as a minute correction to the usual figure of 365 $\frac{1}{4}$, so 365 $\frac{305}{1217}$ = 365 $\frac{1}{4}$ + $\frac{3}{4868}$. The Greeks had an esthetic preference for fractions with a denominator of 1, so Aristarchus divided 4686 by 3 to get 1622 $\frac{2}{3}$, which he then rounded up to 1623. And so, voila: 365 $\frac{1}{4}$ + $\frac{1}{1623}$! For the complete (mind-numbing) calculations, see Tannery in *Mémoires scientifiques,* 2:79–96; Rapisarda, *Censorini De die natali liber,* 229–300; explained by Heath, *Aristarchus of Samos,* 314–15.

The number of days in a year currently is 365.2422. Of all of these, good old Callippus with 365 $\frac{1}{4}$ (365.2500) comes closest, being only .0078 of a day over—or about 11 minutes, 14 seconds. Aristarchus is next with 365 $\frac{1}{4}$ + $\frac{1}{1623}$ = 365.2506, just 0.0084 of a day over—no more than 12 minutes and 6 seconds off. Meton was next with 365 $\frac{5}{19}$ (= 365.2632)—only 30 minutes, 14 seconds over.

4. *Egypt:* For the "year" in Egypt as really a lunar month or the four months of the three Egyptian seasons, see Proclus on *Timaeus* 22b (1.102.26–29 Diehl), citing Eudoxus; Diodorus Siculus 1.26.3–5; Lactantius *Institutes* 2.12.21, citing Varro; Pliny *Natural History* 7.155, 15.12; Plutarch *Numa* 18.6. The Pharaohs Ison and Arminos are found only here, unless Arminos is to be identified with the Armaios of Diodorus 1.64.13 (supposedly the builder of the great pyramid at Memphis) or the Harmais in the king list of Manetho in Josephus *Against Apion* 1.97–98.

5. *Arcadians:* For their "year," see the sources above; also Plutarch *Numa* 18.7; Macrobius *Saturnalia* 1.12.2. Calling the Arcadians "older than the moon" was widespread: Apollonius Rhodius 4.264, with the scholiast, who cites Aristotle; older scholiasts on Aristophanes *Clouds* 398d; Servius on *Georgics* 2.343, citing Cicero's lost speech for M. Fundanius; Ovid *Fasti* 1.469, 2.289–93; Statius *Thebaid* 4.275; Plutarch *Roman Questions* 76 (*Moralia* 282a); Lucian 48 (*Astrology*) 26.

6. *Horus:* A folk etymology is made to the Greek word *hôros* ("season"). For this passage, cf. Diodorus Siculus 1.26; Macrobius *Saturnalia* 1.21.13.

7. *Acarnanians:* See Plutarch *Numa* 18.6; Macrobius *Saturnalia* 1.12.2.

CHAPTER 20: *The Calendar*

There are a number of enjoyable books about the science and history of the calendar and the measurement of time. See David Ewing Duncan, *The Calendar: The 5000-Year Struggle to Align the Clock and the Heavens—And What Happened to the Missing Ten Days* (London: Fourth Estate, 1998); E. G. Richards, *Mapping Time: The Calendar and Its History* (New York: Oxford University Press, 1999); Bonnie Blackburn and Leofranc Holford-Strevens, *The Oxford Companion to the Year* (Oxford: Oxford University Press, 1999); Duncan Steel, *Marking Time: The Epic Quest to Invent the Perfect Calendar* (New York:

J. Wiley, 2000); Leofranc Holford-Strevens, *The History of Time: A Very Short Introduction* (Oxford: Oxford University Press, 2005).

On the Roman calendar, see Agnes K. Michels, *The Calendar of the Roman Republic* (Princeton: Princeton University Press, 1967); H. H. Scullard, *Festivals and Ceremonies of the Roman Republic* (London: Thames and Hudson, 1981); Robert Hannah, *Greek and Roman Calendars: Constructions of Time in the Classical World* (London: Duckworth, 2005).

1. *Ferentinum, Lavinium:* The calendar at Ferentium is unknown. Lavinium had a calendar of 374 days divided into thirteen months, according to Augustine *City of God* 15.12.

2. *Licinius Macer,* etc.: Censorinus lists his sources, most of them now lost, of which Varro, and Suetonius's *On the Year of the Romans* (*De anno Romanorum*) were the most important. Some of the extant sources for the Roman calendar and its history are Livy 1.19; Ovid *Fasti* 1.27–44; Macrobius *Saturnalia* 1.12–16; Plutarch *Numa* 18–19. See also Aulus Gellius 3.16.16, Julius Solinus 1.39–44; Servius on *Georgics* 1.43.

3. *March:* March was the original first month of the Roman calendar, and Quintilis (July), Sextilis (August), September, October, November, and December, as their names imply, were the fifth through tenth. January and February were added at the end to complete the winter cycle. At some early date, the beginning of the year was marked from January, as implied by the name (see below). However, consuls and others continued to take up their offices on 1 March until 153 BC, when the beginning of the civil year was definitively moved to 1 January (Livy *Periocha* 47 = Cassiodorus *Chronica* AUC 601). See (besides the sources above) Cicero *Laws* 2.54; Ovid *Fasti* 2.47–49, 3.75, 3.135–36; Plutarch *Roman Questions* 19 (*Moralia* 268b); Varro *On the Latin Language* 6.33; Festus 136 (Lindsay).

4. *355 days:* 12 lunar months add up to 354.367 days = 354 days, 8 hours, 48 minutes.

6. *Terminalia:* The festival of Terminus, the Roman god of boundaries. See Ovid *Fasti* 2.638–84.

Refugium: A festival that grew out of a misreading of the ancient calendar. The archaic calendar abbreviation QRCF, Q(*uando*) R(*ex*) C(*omitiavit*) F(*as*),

"When the king made the gathering place sacrifice," was interpreted as *Q(uando) R(ex) C(omitio) F(ugerit)*, "When the king fled the gathering place." See Ovid *Fasti* 2.685–865; Plutarch *Roman Questions* 63 (*Moralia* 279c–d); Festus 311 (Lindsay). The *rex sacrorum*, the religious "king," left after the legendary expulsion of the Etruscan king Tarquin the Proud (510 BC), had to run from the Forum after making the sacrifice on this day.

8. *Julius Caesar:* Caesar's reform of the calendar with the aid of the astronomer Sosigenes marked one of the most important advances in measuring time. See Pliny *Natural History* 2.35, 18.211; Suetonius *Julius Caesar* 40; Plutarch *Julius Caesar* 59; Ovid *Fasti* 3.155–66; Appian *Civil War* 2.154; Dio Cassius 43.26. For the Nones and Ides, see also the glossary above, under "Ides."

Caesar's calendar remained in effect in Europe until 1582. Since the year is a fraction less than 365 1/4 days, a new adjustment had to be made by Pope Gregory XIII (1502–85). For a wonderful children's book based on this unlikely subject, see Abner Shimony, *Tibaldo and the Hole in the Calendar* (New York: Copernicus, 1998).

445 days: And so the longest civil year in western history.

10. *Nones and Ides:* A handy rhyme:

In March, July, October, May,

The Ides are on the fifteenth day,

The Nones on the seventh; all months besides

Have two less days for Nones and Ides.

Leap Day: The day was inserted between six days before the Kalends of March (23 February) and five days before the Kalends of March (24 February) and was unnumbered, hence its name *bissextum* ("sixth twice"). Technically, 24 February has been Leap Day in most countries that used a Roman calendar. Thus Saints' Days that normally fell on 24–28 February were celebrated a day later in leap years. For example, St. Matthias's day moved between 24 and 25 February, and in 1969 his day was finally moved to 14 May. Only in 2000 did the European Union officially make 29 February Leap Day.

See Alan Edouard Samuel, *Greek and Roman Chronology: Calendars and Years in Classical Antiquity* (Munich: Beck, 1972) and E. J. Bickerman, *Chronology of the Ancient World*, rev. ed. (London: Thames and Hudson, 1980).

1. *Varro calls the "historical":* Varro's tripartite division, using Greek terms, was taken over by Vico in *The New Science* preface.

The chronology of the Mythical Age thus runs:

c. 2376 BC: Ogyges and the Flood

c. 1976 BC: Inachus at Argos

1290 BC, 1193 BC, 1183 BC, or 1171 BC: Trojan War

776 BC: First Olympics

2. *Ogygius (Ogygos, Ogyges):* For the legendary king of Thebes, see Varro *On Agriculture* 3.1.2–3: Pausanias 9.5.1.

Inachus: River god and father of Io. See Virgil *Aeneid* 7.372, 7.792; Horace *Odes* 2.3.21, 3.19.1; Ovid *Metamorphoses* 1.583; Plutarch *Theseus* 4; Apollodorus *Library* 2.13; Pausanias 2.15.4–5. For a different story of the first flood, see chapter 4.6.

‹*From then to the Trojan War was about 800 years,*›: The text is missing the difference between 1,600 and 400 plus 400 years.

6. *this year . . . is the 1014th since the first Olympiad:* The passage, in which Censorinus gives the current year in all the major systems of the ancient world and ties it to the astronomical event of the heliacal rising of Sirius, is one of the most important for establishing the chronology of the ancient world.

Parilia: Festival of the god (or goddess) Pares. Originally a purification of the herds, with a complex ritual involving leaping through bonfires. See Cicero *On Divination* 2.98, Varro *On Agriculture* 2.1.9; *Latin Language* 6.15; Virgil *Georgics* 3.1 (and Servius's commentary); Ovid *Fasti* 4.721–862; *Metamorphoses* 14.774–75; Dionysius of Halicarnassus 1.88.3; Livy 4.2.1; Pliny *Natural History* 19.154; Plutarch *Romulus* 12. See also Festus 248 (Lindsay).

9. *Nabonnasar:* The era began on 27 February 747 BC. The astronomer

Ptolemy of Alexandria calculated dates from the start of the reign of King Nabonnasar of Babylon, since his records contained the earliest astronomical observations available to him. See *Ptolemy's Almagest,* trans. G. J. Toomer (Princeton: Princeton University Press, 1998), 166 (3.7 = 254 Heiberg).

10. *Thoth:* See above, note 18.10. Since the Egyptian year contained 365 days and made no provision for leap years, it fell behind one day every four years. See Rapisarda's edition for the calculations.

which fell this year on June 25: And so the book was presented to Caerellius after this date, but probably before 28 August 238.

CHAPTER 22: *Months*

For the astronomical and zodiacal months, see Geminus 1.1–8, 8.1–5 (Heath, *Greek Astronomy,* 126–27, 136). For the Roman calendar, see Ovid's *Fasti,* an uncompleted epic poem (January–May) using the historical, mythical, and religious events of the calendar as a framework for literary brilliance.

2. *The lunar month is the space of time between new moons:* Censorinus is referring to the "synodic" lunar month (from Greek *syn* + *odos,* "on the same path"), when the first thin crescent of the new moon can be seen after sunset. The time is not quite constant, since the moon's orbit is elliptical and tilted to the plane of the ecliptic (the earth's orbit around the sun). Meanwhile, the earth is orbiting the sun, and there are perturbations in both orbits. Therefore, the exact periods between new moons depends on the position of earth and moon in their orbits, as well as the latitude and longitude of the observer. The range is from about 29.27 to 29.83 days.

6. *Alba,* etc.: See above, chapter 20.1.

9. *March,* etc.: For the names of the months, see Varro *Latin Language* 6.33–34; Macrobius *Saturnalia* 1.12.8–36. March (*Martius*) is named after Mars, as god of battle who presides over spring, the beginning of the campaigning season. Macrobius *Saturnalia* 1.12.8 claims that April (*Aprilis*) is really *Aphrilis* and comes from Greek *aphros* ("foam"), from which Aphrodite was born. Varro's etymology of *Aprilis* from *aperit* ("opens") is no better, but the

actual etymology is unknown and was probably borrowed from a pre-Italic language. For the others, Varro is mostly right. May (*Maius*) is probably the name of an ancient god (cf. Maia), but the name really does mean "greater" (*mag-ios*) and is therefore is connected with *maiores* "the greater ones; the ancestors." June (*Iunius*) comes from *Juno*, and has nothing to do with *juniores.* January is the month of Janus, the two-faced god of openings, and February is from *februa* ("expiatory offerings") (see Varro *Latin Language* 6.13).

15. *Lupercalia:* 15 February. One of the most bizarre of Roman festivals. In the Lupercal, the cave where the she-wolf was supposed to have suckled Romulus and Remus, the Romans sacrificed goats and dogs. Then the blood was smeared on the faces of two boys, who gave a ritual laugh, and the blood was wiped off with wool dipped in milk. Men in special religious associations, called Luperci, wearing only loin cloths made from the skins of the sacrificed goats, ran around Rome striking women as well as men with the goat-skin thongs. See Ovid *Fasti* 2.19–36, 267–452; Dionysius of Halicarnassus 1.32.3–5, 1.80.1; Varro *Latin Language* 6.13, 6.34; Valerius Maximus 2.2.9; Plutarch *Romulus* 21; *Antony* 12; *Julius Caesar* 61; Servius on *Aeneid* 8.341.

17. *Afterwards, many emperors changed the names of certain months:* So Nero tried to rename April "Neroneus" (Tacitus *Annals* 16.12; Suetonius *Nero* 55). Domitian called September "Germanicus" and October "Domitianus" (Martial 9.1.1–4; Suetonius *Domitian* 13; Macrobius *Saturnalia* 1.12.36–37; Plutarch *Numa* 19.7). Commodus renamed all the months after his various self-awarded titles: "Amazonius, Invictus, Felix, Pius, Lucius, Aelius, Aurelius, Commodus, Augustus, Herculeus, Romanus, Exsuperatorius" (Cassius Dio 73.15.3; *Historia Augusta, Commodus* 11.8–9; Herodian 1.14.90; *Suda* K 2007 "Komodos" (150.18 Adler).

CHAPTER 23: *Days*

Censorinus's source is Varro's "On Days," part of his *Antiquities of Human Things*; Macrobius *Saturnalia* 1.3.2–8; Aulus Gellius 3.2.1–11; cf. Pliny *Natural*

History 2.188. On the definition of "day" and when it begins, see Geminus 6.1–2; Servius on *Aeneid* 5.738, 6.255, 10.216; Plutarch *Roman Questions* 84 (*Moralia* 284c–f); Hyginus *Astronomy* 4.9; *Digest of Justinian* 2.12.8.

6. *sundial:* See Pliny *Natural History* 2.187 (attributing the invention to Anaximenes) and 7.212–15 (on Rome); Vitruvius 9.8.1.

ante meridiem: The origin of our abbreviation "AM"; "PM" is *post meridiem*. See Aulus Gellius 17.2.10 on the Twelve Tables, the oldest Roman laws.

CHAPTER 24: *Hours*

On these old names for the times of day, see Varro *Latin Language* 6.4–7, 7.77–79; Macrobius *Saturnalia* 1.3.12–16.

4. *Plautus: Amphitryo* 275. Ennius op. inc. 29 (132, 763 Skutsch). Virgil *Eclogues* 8.30, 10.77.